THE SCOTTISH
COUNTRY HOUSE

James Knox

Photographs by James Fennell

THE VENDOME PRESS

NEW YORK

CONTENTS

Introduction

THE SCOTS ARE KNOWN FOR THEIR HARDINESS, AND THIS TALE OF TEN houses is one of remarkable longevity played out against the backdrop of Scottish history. With one exception, all of the houses are still lived in either by the families who built them or by those who have owned them for generations. The palm for the longest tenure must go to the Munros, who have inhabited the lands of Foulis since the eleventh century. The exception is Dumfries House, which passed out of private ownership in 2007 and is run by a charitable trust presided over by the Prince of Wales, who led a consortium of donors to save it for the nation. The house and estate are now the catalyst for regeneration in an acutely deprived district of Scotland. Country houses have always been hubs of economic activity but never more so than today, when tourism has been added to the traditional mix of farming and sport. Nowhere is this more evident than at Ballindalloch Castle, where Aberdeen Angus graze, golf is played, salmon are caught, and the lady laird pens best-selling books inspired by the house.

Many of the houses are touchstones of history. The 1603 Union of the Crowns, the rise of Presbyterianism, the seventeenth-century civil war between Royalists and Parliamentarians, the 1707 Union of Parliaments, the Jacobite 1745 Rebellion, the blaze of the Enlightenment, the High Victorian era of prosperity, and the current debate on Scottish independence have all played out in these houses. And the dominant roles have not always been held by men. Families also benefited from the influence of formidable women, a number of whom, under Scottish law, inherited titles, chiefdoms, or the house and estate in their own right. Anne, Duchess of Buccleuch, is the most notable example, but the title and inheritance have also passed through the senior female line in the Dalyell and Munro families.

The houses' historical significance is equaled by their aesthetic importance. The architectural story begins at the turn of the seventeenth century with the Jacobean House of the Binns and concludes at the turn of the twentieth with the Belle Époque Monzie Castle. Milestones passed along the way are the cutting-edge classicism of Balcaskie, the French château–inspired Drumlanrig, the baroque splendor of Arniston, the rationalist planning of Bowhill, and the full-blown Scottish Baronial of Lochinch. In one form or another, each expresses the particular genius of the Scots—their adventurousness and conservatism, their inventiveness and craftsmanship, their sensuality and severity, their rootedness.

Geology is the bedrock of architecture, and nowhere more so than in the rugged terrain of Scotland. A point made by Mrs. Eleanor Dalyell of the House of the Binns,

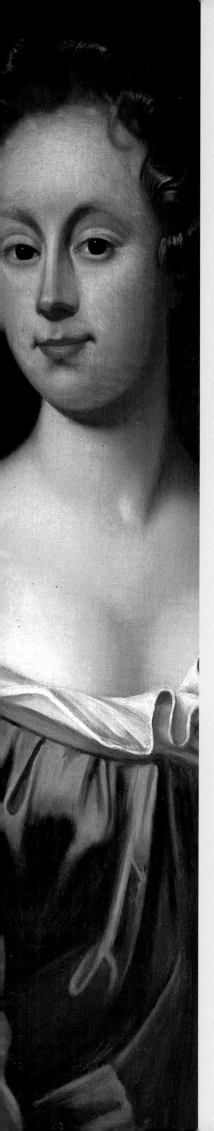

who would gesture with a sweep of her arm toward a volcanic outcrop incorporated into the foundations, declaring it "the living rock on which our ancient house was built." The availability of stone suitable for building produced some dazzling effects such as the pink sandstone of Drumlanrig and Dumfries House; in contrast, the rubble walls of Ballindalloch and Foulis are covered with lime harling for protection against the weather, presenting a more subdued appearance, typical of Scottish vernacular architecture.

The Scots engaged with their sublime landscape long before the cult of the picturesque awoke the rest of Britain to the pleasures of a good view. When the high wall that had obscured the old house of Arniston was demolished in 1726, men came running to the dying laird, who was seated reading in his favorite spot—the hollowed-out trunk of an ancient ash tree—to tell him the news that the sea could now be seen from the windows. Elsewhere, the shutters had long been thrown open. Precedents stretch back to the Renaissance of houses aligned on distant prospects; however, the first master of all he surveyed was Sir William Bruce, who treated architecture and landscape as one, manipulating both on a gigantic scale. His remodeled Balcaskie is built upon an escarpment, exaggerating its dominance over the vista toward the sea and his chosen eye-catcher—an island in the Firth of Forth.

The Scots loved verticality in architecture. Tower houses, such as Ballindalloch and Monzie, stayed in fashion long after their original defensive purpose had declined. Writer and spy Daniel Defoe noted on his 1706 travels the "lairds houses built all castle-wise." These archetypal Scottish buildings, often quite modest in scale, suited even the poorest laird, offering protection, comfort, and status. The grandees were just as attached to their enormous castles, which since the Renaissance, when the French and Scottish courts were allied through marriage, had taken their cue from the trophy châteaux of Fontainebleau and the Loire valley. Only twenty years before Defoe's mission to Scotland, the Duke of Queensberry had cleared the old defensive site of Drumlanrig in Dumfriesshire to build a castle inspired by French mannerism, Renaissance geometry, and modern Scottish baroque. This was no hankering after the past but a proclamation of current power and status springing from deep foundations.

Two of Scotland's most original architects had a hand in Drumlanrig. The first, Sir William Bruce, looked over preliminary plans drawn up in the 1670s, and the second, James Smith, was appointed by the Duke of Queensberry in 1686 to finalize the design and complete the building. Bruce's influence is found in the baroque motifs borrowed from his masterworks—Kinross House and the Royal Palace of Holyroodhouse. A Renaissance man of wide horizons, well traveled, particularly in France, and versed in mathematics, statecraft, and architecture, Bruce introduced modern European classicism to Scotland. The coroneted clock tower above the entrance at Drumlanrig pays homage to the crowned cupola on the entrance front at Holyroodhouse, while the giant order of classical columns, only the second in Scotland, echoes the prototype at Kinross House. James Smith, who had worked on both buildings as Bruce's protégé, and later at Holyroodhouse in his own right as Overseer of Royal Works, was responsible for importing these up-to-the minute flourishes to remote Dumfriesshire. He, too, was an architect with a seasoned eye for the innovative. As a young man he had studied Renaissance architecture in Italy, returning home to Scotland around 1670 with a sheaf of drawings, including a group derived from Palladio's buildings in the Veneto.

Between them, Bruce and Smith designed a series of purely classical houses—including Kinross, Newhailes, Hopetoun, and Dalkeith Palace—that launched the style in Scotland. Smith's influence stretched further afield. Fellow Scot Colen Campbell, whose practice in England established him as the pioneer of Palladian architecture in Britain, acquired Smith's drawings of Palladian prototypes. Campbell acknowledged his debt by hailing Smith in his *Vitruvius Britannicus* as "the most experience'd Architect of that Kingdom."

The work of Scotland's classical architects, particularly that of the Adam brothers, has proved one of the country's most significant exports to Europe and America. The Adam family practice was established by William Adam, born in 1689, who was described by his son-in-law John Clerk of Eldin as "a man of vigourous and enterprising genius." The next in line of descent from Bruce and Smith, he made his reputation in the 1720s with a group of potent baroque houses, one of which is Arniston. William Adam was a leading figure in the dawning Scottish Enlightenment; his home in Niddry's Wynd in the medieval city of Edinburgh was acknowledged as "the resort of men of genius and literature." The large family dwelling brimmed with offspring, which added to its charm, as the children—including the future architects John, Robert, and James—were noted for their "uninterrupted cordiality . . . conciliating manners [and] accomplishments." They brought home their own friends and contemporaries, who, like them, were to shape the modern world, such as David Hume, Adam Smith, and James Hutton, turning the drawing room at Niddry's Wynd into one of the most brilliant and congenial salons of the eighteenth century.

When William Adam, or "old stone and lime," as he was known to his children, died in 1748, his sons took over the practice. Arniston was completed and—with the help of one of their father's patrons—the commission for Dumfries House was won. Robert Adam went on to become the idol of British neoclassicism, imprinting his style on country houses and cities alike, not least on Edinburgh's New Town, which spread below the castle-topped acropolis, earning the city's sobriquet Athens of the North. But the Scots' love of castles was embedded in Adam's psyche. Throughout his life he loved to sketch imaginary castles in wild surroundings, and in the 1770s he realized a series of contemporary castles, deploying minimalist Roman motifs in restless, sometimes romantic compositions such as Culzean Castle, perched on the cliffs of Ayrshire's coast. Although in the same county as Dumfries House, stylistically a romantic chasm divides the two.

Adam's pupil John Paterson, architect of the castle block at Monzie, carried the torch into the nineteenth century. But it was the author Sir Walter Scott who turned the revival of castle building into a craze. The foundations were laid in his sensational 1814 novel *Waverley*, an enthralling tale of the Jacobite '45 Rebellion that includes a detailed description of a Highland tower house and its estate. Two years later, Scott went on to build his own version of the house at Abbotsford in the Borders, sharing an architect, William Atkinson, with his close friend and neighbor, the fourth Duke of

Buccleuch, who was extending Bowhill. A comparison of the two houses reveals Scott's originality: whereas the docile duke was content with unassuming Regency additions, Scott dismissed his architect's "Gothic" design in favor of his own "old fashioned Scotch stile [with] notch't Gable ends & all manner of bartizans [projecting towers] . . ." This revolutionary style, he predicted, would lead to "an entirely new line of architecture."

His invention, now known as Scottish Baronial, took the country by storm. Through the prism of literature and architecture, Scott had healed the wounds of history. A touch of showmanship was all part of the cure: his staging of George IV's triumphant visit to Edinburgh in 1822 saw the Hanoverian monarch dressed head to toe in tartan. The symbols of a vanished Highland culture became acceptable to the British. The Earl of Stair, head of the Dalrymple dynasty of arch Whigs and unionists, chose as the style for Lochinch, his new castle on his lowland estate, one of the most bravura examples of Scottish Baronial, bristling with bartizans, turrets, and the "high steep roofs and narrow gables" of the Jacobite tower house Scott described in *Waverley*.

Robert Lorimer's beautifully crafted reconstruction of Monzie tower house brings the story of Scottish country house architecture into the twentieth century. Baronialism had been transmuted by the Arts and Crafts movement into a simplified style of castle building and reconstruction with an emphasis on materials, function, detailing, massing, and form—eternal principles of architecture that Lorimer was to deploy to brilliant effect in his Scottish National War Memorial at Edinburgh Castle, setting him upon a plinth of greatness along with his fellow architects in this book.

The glory of Scottish country houses is not just their architecture but their contents, which add layers of personality to the interiors: tactile evidence of generations past and present with their collections of furniture, china, books, ancestral charters, kilts, portraits, *objets de vertu*, and military and sporting trophies, all summed up by Kathleen Dalyell, who refers to the contents of The Binns as "pure hotch potch, some good taste, some bad." The ducal treasure houses of Drumlanrig and Bowhill are exceptions and so too is the Adam-designed Dumfries House, one of the most complete documents of Enlightenment taste in Scotland, with all of its original Chippendale and Scottish rococo furniture intact.

In 2007 the imminent dispersal of this unique collection along with the sale of the house and the estate sparked one of the most dramatic rescues in the history of British architectural conservation. A handful of activists based in Ayrshire and London (SAVE Britain's Heritage) had less than three months to save a house that until then had been totally private, was located in a neglected part of Scotland, and had a price tag of over £40 million. Within weeks, millions were pledged from private sources and applications were drawn up for grants from government heritage bodies. In the local town of Cumnock, people queued to sign a petition to save Dumfries House. But there was still a mountain to climb.

And the man who scaled it was the Prince of Wales, who became involved after attending a conference organized by his regeneration charity at Holyroodhouse, at which the plight of Dumfries House had been brought up. A secret rescue plan was devised to raise £20 million against a property development on the edge of the estate, which would bridge the funding gap, but with just four weeks before the

Christie's auction, the furniture was already being crated up for removal to the London salesroom.

Frenzied negotiations continued in London and Edinburgh, which, thanks to the Prince of Wales, resulted in the government agencies' confirmation of their grants for the house, and agreement on the land deal. But the situation was still so tenuous that the removal vans, loaded with Chippendale, were dispatched to London and had already reached the Lake District some three hours later when they were recalled. The contract was finalized that weekend and the news announced two weeks before the planned sale.

The Prince of Wales held a celebration party at Dumfries House on what would have been the first day of the Christie's sale. Afterward, he visited Cumnock, where townspeople lined up to thank their "Prince Charming." A local resident spoke for all when she told a reporter: "The town has been in terrible decline since the closure of the coal mines, but Dumfries House will bring new industry." She was right. House and estate are now humming with life—a major supermarket runs the farm, there is an education center, a café, and a bed and breakfast; the house itself has been brilliantly restored and the property development is under way. The Prince of Wales's brave decision to rescue Dumfries House has shown that great art can bring prosperity as well as joy. And that Scottish country houses lie at the heart and soul of the nation.

PAGE 1: *Pewter corridor, Dumfries House.*

PAGES 2–3: *Entrance front, Dumfries House.*

PAGES 4–5: *Archive Room, Bowhill.*

PAGE 6: *Portrait of Louisa, Countess of Stair, by Rudolf Lehmann, Lochinch Castle.*

PAGE 7: *Portrait of John, second Duke of Argyll, by Sir Godfrey Kneller, Drumlanrig.*

PAGE 8: *Portrait of Miss Seymour, sister-in-law of Sir Robert Munro, Foulis Castle.*

PAGE 9: *Portrait of Alexander Grant by Richard Waitt, 1725, Ballindalloch Castle.*

PAGE 10: *Portrait of Grizzel Dundas, attributed to Benjamin West, Arniston.*

PAGE 11: *Portrait of fifth Duke of Buccleuch and Queensberry by Sir John Watson Gordon, Bowhill.*

The House of the Binns

WEST LOTHIAN

The prospect of a visit to The Binns by King Charles I had led Dalyell to commission the plasterer, Alexander White . . . to decorate the High Hall and the King's Room with an extravagant program of plasterwork celebrating the Union of the Scottish and English Crowns. King Charles's Scottish tour was truncated at the last minute, but Dalyell's royal salute survives as a glorious expression of his adherence to the newly established "Great Britain."

In 1944 the House of the Binns became the first country house to be handed over by its owners to the National Trust for Scotland, a landmark act of generosity that paved the way for the saving of other important Scottish houses in the difficult years ahead. In addition to its historical and architectural value, other considerations had played a part. "They wanted somewhere near Edinburgh," explains the present laird, Tam Dalyell, "in good condition and with no awkward relations to get in the way. The man with the best claim after me was a distant cousin in America, who had been chosen in 1944 by Franklin Delano Roosevelt as his vice presidential running mate. By the following year, Harry S. Truman had become president of the United States and had a few other things on his mind than an ancient house in West Lothian."

The groundwork had been laid by Tam's formidable mother, Eleanor Dalyell, through whom the family name and title could pass. She and her husband, Colonel Gordon Loch, an outstanding government servant, felt that, as Tam explains, "the property belonged to Scotland." Even as an eleven-year-old boy, he understood and agreed with their high-minded decision, signing the deed of transfer as heir

presumptive in his headmaster's study at prep school, having been made, he recalls, "to sit in the chair over which he had beaten me the night before—with good reason, I might say. It was the only occasion when he lent a boy his fountain pen."

The house, parkland, historic contents, and a significant endowment were gifted to the Trust in return for the Dalyell family's right to carry on living at The Binns and also open it to the public. This responsibility has fallen on the willing shoulders of Tam's wife, Kathleen Dalyell, who has dedicated her working life to the

PRECEDING PAGES: *The "Gothicized" north front (1810–30).*

OPPOSITE: *Scottish sculptor Charles Pilkington Jackson's* Napoleon, *a legendary foe of the Royal Scots Greys, the regiment founded by General Tam Dalyell.*

ABOVE: *The present laird, Tam Dalyell, by Gerald Laing; arrow added by the grandchildren.*

OVERLEAF: *The Laigh (low) Hall, originally two rooms, retains the original Jacobean fireplace, dated 1622.*

ABOVE: *Glimpse of the south (garden) front with original Jacobean dormers.*

BELOW: *Clod of earth symbolizing the family's gift of the house to the National Trust for Scotland. Accompanying photo of the 1946 ceremony with Eleanor Dalyell and young Tam in the background.*

OPPOSITE: *General Tam's Russian boots (perched on a Boulle plinth) and broadsword above the fireplace in the dining room. His Russian stool stands to the left, beneath a portrait of scholar Sir John Dalyell, who taught Charles Darwin natural history.*

OVERLEAF: *The morning room, built out over the courtyard front in 1745.*

upkeep and maintenance of The Binns on a voluntary basis as the Trust's manager.

Kathleen Dalyell once suggested to her mother-in-law that gifting the house to the Trust was essentially a socialist act. "That's not exactly what I had in mind," came the reply. Her son, however, has served as one of the most remarkable socialist politicians of his generation—equal in courage, independence, and single-mindedness to his old foe, Margaret Thatcher, whom he harried over the Falklands War despite his being reviled at the time. "I am inoculated against opprobrium," he says.

Kathleen Dalyell, past chairman of the Royal Commission on the Ancient and Historical Monuments of Scotland, is a passionate advocate for the house, but with one proviso. When asked to name her favorite building in Scotland, she indeed chooses The Binns, though not the romanticized version one sees today but "the original seventeenth-century structure built between 1612 and 1630 by that enterprising merchant, adventurer, civil servant, and spy, Thomas Dalyell."

His first fortune was made as a butter merchant in Edinburgh; his second, from his marriage in 1601 to Janet Bruce, daughter of the Scottish ambassador to London, a key figure in the secret negotiations over James VI of Scotland's proposed accession to the English throne on the death of Elizabeth I. His accession in 1603 saw the Dalyells move to London on the coattails of Janet's influential father, where, as one of the gang of "hungrie Scots," Thomas was granted a lucrative government position. This paid for the purchase in 1612 of his Scottish estate, crowned by a high *binnis*, the old Scottish word for "hill," on which he built the House of the Binns.

Fresh from London, Dalyell, who acted as his own clerk of works, built one of the first modern country houses in Scotland. Its original seventeenth-century appearance was that of an unfortified structure of pleasing symmetry with mullioned windows, pepper-pot roofs, and chic French dormers punctuating the roof line. Everything about this innovative yet modest building proclaimed that a new age of peace and plenty had dawned. One approached through a cobbled courtyard flanked by matching wings housing a brew house, bakehouse, dairy, saddle house, and other buildings serving the estate. The front door opened not onto a defensive spiral stair, but into a reception room with a handsome

chimneypiece of classical design. Upstairs, the state rooms, with views north over the river Forth and south over the Pentland Hills, were decorated with a joyous confection of plasterwork, as though molded from thick icing sugar, on ceilings, friezes, and overmantels, laced with classical heroes, coats of arms, and fruit and flowers in abundance.

The prospect of a visit to The Binns by King Charles I had led Dalyell to commission the plasterer, Alexander White, a master of the Jacobean court style, to decorate the High Hall and the King's Room with

an extravagant program of plasterwork celebrating the Union of the Scottish and English Crowns. King Charles's Scottish tour was truncated at the last minute, but Thomas Dalyell's royal salute survives as a glorious expression of his adherence to the newly established "Great Britain."

His legacy has had a profound impact upon the present laird, Tam Dalyell, who as the local Member of Parliament has gone down in recent history as the most tenacious of all campaigners against the breakup of the union. "My ancestors," he explains, "had played a significant role in the 1603 Union of the Crowns and, throughout The Binns, decorative plasterwork and wood carving display thistles and roses as symbols of this Union. My parents, being staunch Unionists, were always very conscious of their commitment and duty to Great Britain. I imbibed some of this ethos." He did indeed. Tam was instrumental in the defeat of the earliest attempt to establish a Scottish Assembly; and his famous parliamentary "West Lothian Question" (named after his constituency), which asks why Scottish MPs should have the right to vote on English matters when their English colleagues have no say in Scotland, is invoked repeatedly in the fierce debate over Scottish independence.

Although retired from the fray, Tam is unrepentant. "I cannot but be shaped by my ancestors," he says. "They were present and looked down on me from the walls of rooms in daily use and their portraits depicted serious people who had expectations of me. I suppose I was driven by my ancestors to be useful and not to let them down."

One such portrait is the bearded visage of his seventeenth-century namesake, General Tam Dalyell, who as an ardent royalist refused to shave or cut his hair until the Stuart monarchy had been restored to the throne. His giant horn comb is on show to

prove it, as are other relics of his adventurous life, including a pair of Russian cavalry boots and a two-handed sword from his days of fighting for the czar of Russia.

In true Scots' fashion, General Tam cultivated an image of ferocity both to demoralize his enemies and to promote the confidence of kings in his powers of leadership. His life at The Binns reveals a more sophisticated personality with an informed eye for fashionable paneling and paintwork, which can still be seen in the Blue Room. A man of great education and wide travels, he built, as described in his inventory, "locked shelfs wherin is his haill biblothick" behind the paneling in the adjoining "little studie." This rare survival of an early laird's library was also equipped with an alphabetical catalogue and "a ledder for climeing up to the books."

Later Dalyells, who had been made baronets (hereditary knights) by the Stuart king James II, largely respected the seventeenth-century interiors. The handsome Georgian morning room and dining room were built out over the

TOP AND ABOVE: *Tam, ensuring that Scottish independence remains a bone of contention . . . and in dogged pursuit of Mrs. Thatcher. Cartoons by Griffin in the Guardian.*

RIGHT: *General Tam's Blue Room, painted and paneled in the 1680s, concealing earlier decoration.*

OPPOSITE, CLOCKWISE FROM TOP LEFT: *General Tam untrimmed; Colonel Gordon Loch; earlier decoration revealed in the Blue Room; the General's Russian boots.*

1599 THOMAS DALYELL . 1685

"AFTER HE HAD PROCURED HIMSELF A LASTING NAME IN THE WARS,
HERE IT WAS THAT HE RESTED HIS OLD AGE, AND PLEASED
HIMSELF WITH THE CULTURE OF CURIOUS FLOWERS AND PLANTS"
CAMD: BRIT:

courtyard, and the entrance was moved to the north front. Their innate taste reflects the inherited values of the family: high-mindedness, courage, intellect, and enterprise, with a dash of stubbornness and swashbuckling thrown in. There was only one black sheep, labeled by Kathleen Dalyell as "the odious fifth baronet, the gambling and womanising Sir James Dalyell . . . who wanted to make his modest home grander in the Gothic style." He removed the dormer windows from the north front, although they can still be glimpsed on the south, and superimposed the battlements and turrets that give the house its present Gothic veneer.

His pretentiousness still rankles with Kathleen Dalyell, who says: "If I could do away with the battlements, I would." A lively dialogue with the past by the present chatelaine is all part of the remarkable personality of the House of the Binns, which, thanks to the Dalyells, remains at the heart of Scotland's history today.

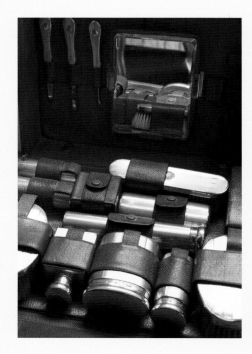

Balcaskie

FIFE

Bruce's remodeling revealed an instinct for symmetry, mass, movement, and form—signs of a baroque architect in the making. His embedding of the old house in the new also advertised a sharp eye for economy, a trait certain to go down well with Scottish earls.

Balcaskie is the story of Scotland's unsung architectural genius, Sir William Bruce (1630–1710), who planted the baroque style in Scotland's dramatic landscape, and with his masterpieces—Kinross House and the Royal Palace of Holyroodhouse—established a vigorous strain of Continental classicism equal to any in northern Europe. This achievement was nurtured at Balcaskie, an unassuming laird's house and estate in Fife that he bought in 1665 as his own seat. His remodeling of the existing house and designs for the landscape, most of which survive, were the testing ground for the evolution of his taste and practices as an architect.

Following Bruce's sale of Balcaskie, the property was eventually bought in 1698 by Sir Thomas Anstruther, scion of an ancient Fife family. Today his descendant Toby Anstruther lives in Balcaskie and is immensely proud of being the guardian of Bruce's remarkable house. Architecture rather than ancestry has always been his primary interest, instilled in him by his architect mother, whose idea of a family holiday was a cultural tour abroad with Banister Fletcher's bible of world architecture to hand; in England it was Nikolaus Pevsner's county guides. In a romantic twist, Toby Anstruther is married to Kate Pevsner, granddaughter of

the architectural historian. "We are very lucky to have such a beautiful house," he says. "It is easy to take history, particularly one's own, for granted, but I never cease to wonder at the quality of what Bruce designed and built, and it is a real privilege to live at Balcaskie. Bruce certainly deserves his place among the greats of Scottish architecture."

By the time Sir William Bruce purchased Balcaskie, he was prospering in the service of the Crown. The younger son of a Perthshire laird, he had begun life as a merchant in Holland and France, the perfect cover for espionage, which

PRECEDING PAGES: *The distinctive bookcases in the library post-date architect William Bruce's original design.*

OPPOSITE: *Detail of the library plasterwork, 1674, executed by George Dunsterfield, one of the craftsmen working for Bruce at the Royal Palace of Holyroodhouse.*

ABOVE: *Fall of Icarus, attributed to de Witt, who also worked at Holyroodhouse.*

OVERLEAF: *The original court was closed in by the entrance front, which was built out between the two gable ends.*

33

led to his involvement in the Restoration of Charles II. A knighthood and government posts followed, but his greatest reward was his appointment in 1667 as collector of fines and property taxes for the Scottish Treasury Commission. A covey of earls presided over the newly established commission, which was responsible for collecting and distributing the king's revenues, not least among themselves. Ruthless yet cultivated, the eleven commissioners set about rebuilding their ancestral seats and lesser houses; more often than not they sought the advice of their gifted tax collector-turned-architect, Sir William Bruce.

His transformation of Balcaskie had shown what he could do. The approach to the house was through a *cour d'honneur* bounded by matching pavilions and screen walls that led into a three-sided entrance court. A wing of the original house formed one side of the court; its pair was a copy by Bruce but with sufficient variation in the windows to signal the difference between ancient and modern. The gable ends of both wings are still visible today, but the entrance court itself was built over in the nineteenth century to create a new entrance front flush with them. At the back of the house, Bruce's design for the new, extended garden front, which concealed elements of the old house behind it, was a steep-roofed, horizontal range of abstract simplicity with a sweep of windows of classical proportions and a doorway into the garden framed by smart mannerist pilasters. Square, towered pavilions, a contemporary French touch, added bulk at each corner of the house. The remodeling revealed an instinct for symmetry, mass, movement, and form—signs of a baroque architect in the making. His embedding of the old house in the new also advertised a sharp eye for economy, a trait certain to go down well with Scottish earls.

Bruce was one of the very first architects in Britain to tie the design of his house to the surrounding untamed landscape; and as this was Scotland, his canvas was immense. He centered Balcaskie on a view of the Bass Rock, a striking volcanic island that emerges some miles out in the Firth of Forth. To lead the eye, he constructed a formal garden of massive stone terraces, French in their ambition and scale, that fall away from the house to a distant avenue of trees, which in turn directs the gaze to the sea and the shimmering eye-catcher beyond. This brilliant effect anticipated by a good forty years or more the cult of the picturesque, which inspired architects to make the best of a good view. His entrance front was aligned with Kellie Castle, a tower house of great antiquity, a mile distant.

Toby Anstruther is fascinated by Bruce's radicalism, taking as an example his *cour d'honneur*, which, if original, is only the third example to have been built in Britain. Although some, including the latest Pevsner guide, have questioned this claim, Toby Anstruther replies: "My instinct tells me that it's consistent with what he would have done. There's a theatricality about it and it also fits

with his love of axes. It presents somewhere to pause before the moment of arrival." No documentary evidence survives to date this part of the building, but Anstruther has applied his own mathematical analysis. "Given the importance of golden sections and classical proportions to Bruce and baroque architecture of the time," he explains, "I superimposed a classic golden section ellipse on the original proportions of the forecourt: the ellipse describes the *cour d'honneur* perfectly and endorses our belief that the outer pavilions and screen walls are by Bruce or at the very least stand on the footprint of his originals. It is, perhaps, no surprise that the drawing room also conforms to this geometry."

Balcaskie was Bruce's stepping stone to architectural greatness. His growing reputation with the Lords Commissioners, and especially Scotland's viceroy, the Earl of Lauderdale, led to his appointment as Surveyor General of Royal Works in Scotland, with the Royal Grant specifically mentioning his "skill in architecture." Previous holders of this post had been responsible for the finances of projects, leaving highly skilled royal master masons in charge of design and building. Bruce's

promotion singles him out as the first actual architect in Scotland.

Bruce did not allow his new post to distract him from his tax-collecting duties. He was a financial as well an architectural wizard and led the syndicate that won the lucrative contract to "farm" the taxes for the rebuilding of Holyroodhouse, thus receiving double payment for his work. One grandee dismissed him as a "teuch [tough] lawyer"; others admired his dynamism: "Your lordship and I," wrote Viscount Tarbet to the Duke of Gordon, "have known him a vigourous little man as could be."

Bruce's reconstruction of the Palace of Holyroodhouse is one of Britain's earliest and finest essays in Continental classicism. But even at the palace there is a royal nod to Balcaskie. Twin Renaissance towers project at either end of the correct classical screen of the entrance front. One tower is genuinely old, the other newly built by Bruce to match, just as he had balanced the composition of Balcaskie with an old and a new wing.

PRECEDING PAGES: *The dining room.*

TOP, ABOVE, AND RIGHT: *Mementos of Anstruthers past.*

ABOVE RIGHT: *Janet, Lady Strange, was a daughter of the house.*

OPPOSITE: *Sir Ralph Anstruther, Comptroller of the Queen Mother's household, in the uniform of the Coldstream Guards.*

OVERLEAF AND FOLLOWING PAGES: *Beyond the green door of the spacious kitchen, statuary in the garden and a side view of turrets and towered pavilions.*

In return, a touch of royal splendor was bestowed on Balcaskie—a suite of sensational plaster ceilings created by the English craftsmen responsible for the decorative scheme at Holyroodhouse. "No doubt on a Friday afternoon," suggests Anstruther, "the team would be shipped over from the port of Leith with Bruce saying, 'If you want to get paid, do some work here.'"

Bruce left Balcaskie in 1685 to start afresh with his next house, Kinross. Since then, Balcaskie has settled down to quiet centuries of ownership by the soldiers, lawyers, public servants, and courtiers who have headed up the Anstruther family. Toby Anstruther inherited from his cousin Sir Ralph, who was the legendary Comptroller of the Queen Mother's household. The family have treated the house with habitual good manners, their only major faux pas being the building over of the entrance court. It is their accumulation of portraits, furniture, and country house clutter that gives the house its patina of history, which has settled gently over William Bruce's revolutionary structure—the first indication of the genius that was to earn him the posthumous title of "chief introducer of architecture to this country."

Drumlanrig

DUMFRIESSHIRE

he third duke was an amiable courtier, charming, diffident, and cultivated—the perfect foil to his free-spirited wife, Kitty Queensberry, who loved to shock. The fourth duke, a distant cousin, was the most famous rake of Georgian England, immortalized as Old Q. He scarcely visited Scotland and felled the woods at Drumlanrig to increase his coffers, provoking the local bard, Robert Burns, to write: "That reptile wears a ducal crown."

PRECEDING PAGES: *The state bedchamber, known as Bonnie Prince Charlie's bedroom, where the Jacobite prince stayed (uninvited) on his retreat north in 1745. The walls are hung with Brussels tapestries.*

RIGHT: *Enfilade leading through the drawing room and anteroom to the state bedchamber.*

OPPOSITE: *Oak staircase installed by the second duke in 1697. A Grand Tourist who fell in love with St Peter's in Rome, he borrowed Bernini's barley-sugar column. The morning room is glimpsed through the doorway.*

OVERLEAF LEFT: *The Queensberry coat of arms and the family crest—a winged heart—emblazoned indoors and out. It represents Robert the Bruce's heart, which, after his death, was taken by the Black Douglas on a crusade.*

OVERLEAF RIGHT: *The anteroom is lined with early-eighteenth-century chairs and a daybed in original velvet coverings.*

An air of antiquity clings to the castle of Drumlanrig and its parkland. "We're literally in Roman territory here," says the Duke of Buccleuch and Queensberry, "as a huge Roman fort was excavated in 2004 just two hundred yards from the castle itself. I feel it rather wonderful that the poor freezing Romans were here in 140 AD and could not have guessed that their successor culture, manifest in Drumlanrig's classical details, would have influenced such an inhospitable corner of the empire fifteen hundred years later." He continues, "I love this thread of history."

A sense of history runs in the family. The first Duke of Queensberry, who had made a fortune in the 1680s as lord high treasurer of Scotland, deliberately chose to rebuild his ancient seat as a swaggering castle bristling with turrets and towers to proclaim the status and lineage of his family, which stretched back to the 1380s and beyond. The family had been raised to the Earldom of Queensberry by Charles I, but had suffered for its loyalty in the civil war between Royalists and Parliamentarians, leaving the next in line, the future Duke of Queensberry, to restore the family's wealth and reputation. He did so in spades. Not only did Queensberry excel at tax gathering, but

he proved a staunch upholder of established Protestantism. The king's pleasure was reflected in Queensberry's rise from Earl to Marquess to Duke of Queensberry in a mere three years. Royal favor came to an abrupt end in 1686, however, when the Catholic James II sacked Queensberry from all government posts.

The duke retired to his estates in Dumfriesshire to oversee the completion of

BELOW: *The north side of the inner courtyard with two of the four staircase towers. Originally an open loggia, it was glazed in the early nineteenth century to form the present entrance hall.*

OPPOSITE: *The swagger of the north entrance front: the staircase was inspired by the sixteenth-century Château de Fontainebleau; the 1682–84 clock tower, by the contemporary cupola of Holyroodhouse.*

OVERLEAF: *The drawing room is hung with family and royal portraits and appointed with eighteenth-century French furniture.*

PAGE 60: *The cabinet of curiosities presented by Louis XIV to Charles II, who gave it to his son the Duke of Monmouth, ancestor of the Buccleuchs.*

PAGE 61, TOP: *The pedimented doorway of the staircase gallery leads into the drawing room;* BOTTOM LEFT: *King William III by Godfrey Kneller;* BOTTOM RIGHT: *Mary of Modena, Queen Consort of James II, by Willem Wissing.*

his new castle. No one actually knows who designed Drumlanrig. A plan drawn up in 1673 by master mason Robert Mylne had been shown to Scotland's leading architect, William Bruce, but then the scent runs cold. By the 1680s, James Smith, who had been trained by Bruce and Mylne, was in charge. He also had a hand in revising the plans. A scribbled note on the back of an old playing card in the charter room at Drumlanrig refers to "draughts [designs] of the house in Mr. Ja. Smith's [hand]."

There is no question that the overall vision behind the building program was the duke's. Described by colleagues at the treasury as imperious and by a contemporary historian as a man who "loved to be absolute, and to direct everything," he did not hesitate to lash Smith if things went wrong. "Tell him," he wrote to the overseer, William Lukup, "I'm very angrie that Ja. Smith can give me noie account of his having agreed for the wrightwork in the Gallerie. And till that be done he cannot expect Ill be pleased. Its still his way to putt off and delay things, which displeases me and injures him."

Drumlanrig is built on a palimpsest of castles. The stately quadrangle with its four corner stair turrets echoes the ghostly outline of the sixteenth-century "palace and castle" that was demolished to make way for it. However, a rigid geometry derived from an Italian Renaissance palace was imposed on the plan. This structure had already been applied to another prodigal building in Scotland, George Heriot's Hospital in Edinburgh, begun in 1628. In outline, the two buildings bear strong similarities, but there the comparison ends. Heriot's dominates Edinburgh's townscape with all the dignity and sobriety of a Presbyterian Divine. Drumlanrig, in contrast, with its stretched towers, giant classical order, coroneted clock tower, and—*pièce de résistance*—tightly controlled horseshoe staircase, all dressed in pink sandstone, the texture of damask, summons up a mannered Scottish nobleman at the court of François I's Château de Fontainebleau.

The Scots, like their old allies the French, had a long tradition of building castles for display rather than defense. James V remodeled the palaces of Falkland and Linlithgow in the up-to-date Renaissance style of the châteaux of the Loire, doing so in honor of his new bride, the daughter of François I. The tradition was kept alive through Grand Tours to France, such as that of Queensberry's son in 1682, and through the dissemination of pattern books. The engraving of Fontainebleau that Smith used at Drumlanrig is from Jacques Androuet du Cerceau's *Les plus excellents bastiments de France* (1576–79). No wonder the clique of aristocrats made rich after the Restoration by their positions as treasury commissioners led them to revive the style, transforming their archaic seats into symmetrical yet pinnacled châteaux "of noble silhouette." But only their lord high treasurer, having repaired his family's fortunes after the civil war, had the panache

to build himself a brand-new castle, set high on its defensive site, proclaiming for miles around: "We're Ancient. We're Powerful. And We're Back!"

The interior was planned along contemporary baroque lines, with an enfilade of state rooms on the *piano nobile* and private apartments on the ground floor. An open loggia led from the entrance front into the courtyard; above the loggia ran the long gallery for the display of family portraits.

The second Duke of Queensberry built a career to match the scale of Drumlanrig. He dominated Scottish politics for a generation and went on to transform the political landscape of Great Britain by steering the 1707 Act of Union through the Scottish Parliament. The Jacobites, led by Bonnie Prince Charlie, took their revenge in the 1745 Rebellion by occupying Drumlanrig on their march north from Preston, leaving the house "in a sad pickle," as the terrified factor reported to the third duke, concluding, "May God grant there may never again be such guests here." The duke, who was safely tucked up in London, was an amiable courtier, charming, diffident, and cultivated—the perfect foil to his free-spirited wife, Kitty Queensberry, who loved to shock. The fourth duke, a

distant cousin, was the most famous rake of Georgian England, immortalized as Old Q. He scarcely visited Scotland and felled the woods at Drumlanrig to increase his coffers, provoking the local bard, Robert Burns, to write: "That reptile wears a ducal crown."

Old Q died without heirs in 1810, and the dukedom and its Drumlanrig estates passed through the female line to the dukes of Buccleuch. The present duke, sitting in the morning room, part of the first duke's private apartments on the ground floor, muses on the last two Queensberrys' contributions to the family: "The third duke and his wife were great supporters of the opera, particularly John Gay, who revolutionized our approach to the art form. In fact, he dedicated *The Beggar's Opera* to Kitty Queensberry. His next work, *Polly*, was banned by the king. Kitty made a nuisance of herself and she was banned too—from Court. She wrote to the king saying she was thrilled, as Court was so boring."

He admits that "Old Q wasn't a very good prototype. He is the one who was against the trend." By the time of his death, Drumlanrig was in a ruinous state: "The roof was leaking and needed a major overhaul." The improvements were overseen by the writer Sir Walter Scott, a

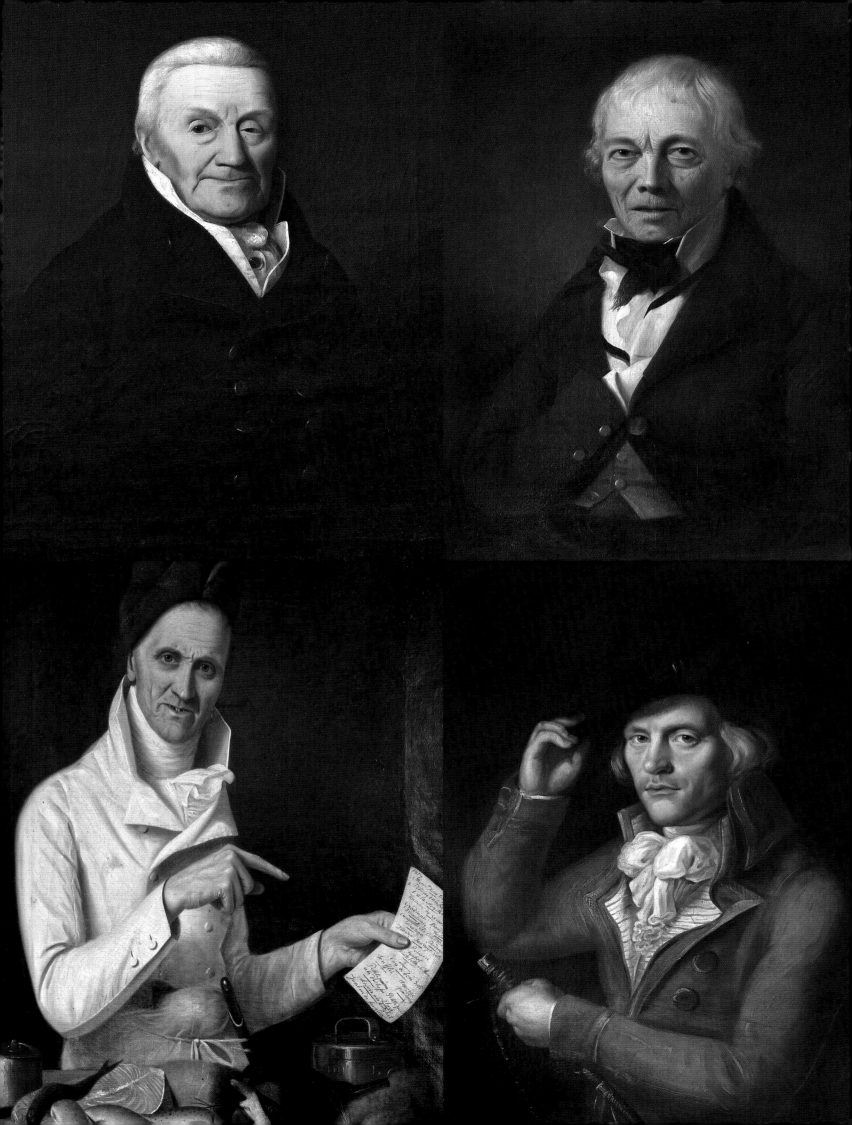

BELOW: Southeast view of the pinnacled roofscape.

OPPOSITE TOP: The east terrace was restored as a topiary garden in 1978 following the 1738 plan.

OPPOSITE BOTTOM LEFT: Gothic undercroft of the north entrance front.

OPPOSITE BOTTOM RIGHT: Carved doorway on the south garden front.

guardian and mentor to the fifth Duke of Buccleuch and Queensberry.

The only major changes were the division of the long gallery into bedrooms and the creation of the dining room out of a portion of the stair hall and a smaller eating room; at a later date the open loggia was enclosed to become the hall. The Buccleuchs came to love the house. "They made it comfortable yet didn't wreck it," says the duke. Indeed, the family greatly enriched the house in the twentieth century when their principal Scottish seat, Dalkeith Palace, coincidentally also designed by James Smith, was closed up after World War I. As a result, its superb collection of furniture, dating from the same period as Drumlanrig, was installed, creating the atmospheric interiors on view today.

Much of the family's enjoyment of the house was rooted in its proximity to the grouse moors. Old leather-bound game books in the hall record thousands of birds shot in the years before World War I, when the house enjoyed a Victorian and Edwardian heyday. The duke's parents revived the tradition in the 1950s and '60s. "For three or four weeks of every summer," he says, " it was one long shooting party with a rota of guests staying up to a week at a time." The present duke no longer shoots. "Do you know, it's just not my thing." But he cares passionately about the past, present, and future of Drumlanrig and its surrounding landscape. And with good reason. "I challenge anyone," he says, "not to fall in love with Scotland after setting eyes on Drumlanrig."

Arniston

MIDLOTHIAN

1 5 5 6

OPVS · VITÆ
CHRISTVS ·

VIVE · VT · VIVAS ·

GEORGE. DVNDAS.
of DVNDAS.

his hospitable chamber, known as the Oak Room, was the setting for many a drinking session with the lord president and his cronies, who sat out on the veranda with hogsheads of claret "getting slockened" while admiring the vista, also designed by Adam, which culminated in a cascade.

"My love for this house," says the lady laird, Althea Dundas-Bekker, "is all tied up with my love of Scottish history, precipitated as a child by seeing the film *Bonnie Prince Charlie* starring David Niven. My parents were very squashing. And it came as a bit of a shock to discover that the Dundases were on the winning side."

Throughout the eighteenth century, her ancestors had been at the heart of the political and legal establishment. One son of the house, Henry Dundas, was even hailed as "the uncrowned King of Scotland." Indeed, at the time of the 1745 Rebellion, the head of the family, Lord Arniston, was a judge on the Court of Session (Scotland's Supreme Court) while his son, the solicitor general, was engaged in organizing opposition to the rebels, who had occupied Edinburgh, though not the castle. No wonder Bonnie Prince Charlie had his eye on Arniston, a mere fifteen miles away, leading the isolated chatelaine, Lady Arniston, to write to her stepson, the solicitor general: "It is positively given out our houses are to be burnt . . . in short we are to be ruined. . . . God protect you and deliver us from these distresses."

Deliverance came in 1746 with the defeat of Bonnie Prince Charlie at the Battle of Culloden, the final blow to Jacobite hopes

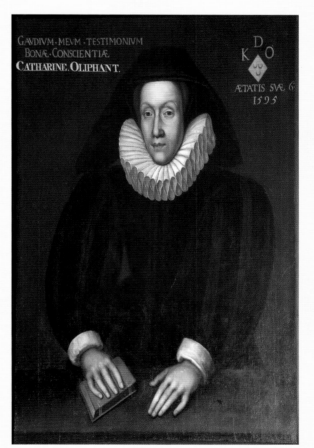

GAVDIVM·MEVM·TESTIMONIVM BONÆ·CONSCIENTIÆ CATHARINE·OLIPHANT.

D
K O
ÆTATIS SVÆ 6
1595

in Scotland, securing Hanoverian rule and with it the Dundas dynasty well into the nineteenth century.

The lands of Arniston, which originally belonged to the Templars, were acquired in 1571 by George Dundas, a younger son of an ancient line, and his spirited second wife, Katherine Oliphant, who insisted on its purchase to provide for their new-born son, James. A tower house of unknown date was

recorded on the site in the early seventeenth century, which became the home of the young James Dundas, who went on to have a distinguished career as a public servant, agricultural reformer, and philosopher. His combination of brains, originality, and energy marked out the Dundases and were the rungs of the family's nimble ascent to power and influence.

For the first hundred years or so, the family occupied James Dundas's tower house, a U-shaped structure constituting the footprint of three sides of the present house. Work on a new building was begun in 1727 by his great-grandson Robert Dundas, who over the course of his career held a royal flush of legal positions, crowned by the lord presidency of the Court of Session.

His choice of architect was William Adam, son of an architect-builder, who was described by a kinsman as "a man . . . who, at an early period of his life, has established himself as the universal architect of his country." By 1727 Adam, revealing a sound grasp of the latest architectural trends emanating from London, had already completed three important commissions within easy reach of Arniston, the most notable being the remodeling of William Bruce's Hopetoun House into a swaggering baroque palace for Dundas's political ally the Earl of Hopetoun. No such fireworks are apparent as one approaches Arniston: its entrance front is a sober composition dominated by a giant ionic portico supporting a richly carved pediment; the flanking colonnades and pavilions complete the picture of a correct classical mansion.

Step inside, however, and one realizes that Adam's unassuming front was the drop curtain for the real drama of the house: his astonishing double-height entrance hall, inspired by Vanbrugh's marble hall at Castle Howard. Adam understood that theatrical

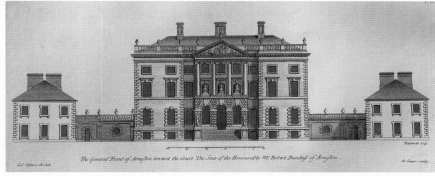

effect was the mainspring of the baroque. His "chief object," he stated, was "to ensure that Architecture be expressed at first view." And his hall at Arniston makes one gasp: giant Corinthian pilasters stretch skyward, supporting vaults and ceiling alive with stucco applied by German craftsman Josef Enzer, who spent six years summoning up an arcadia of gods, birds, flowers, and fruit. Adam was not only a showman but also a master of mood. His library, discovered in the very eaves of the house, is a room of quiet beauty, with richly carved paneling, elegant stucco ornamentation (also by Enzer), and terra-cotta busts bought for the room in Italy by the lord president's son, another Robert Dundas, while on holiday from studying law at Utrecht in the 1730s.

One of the treasures of the library was a copy of the Solemn League of the Covenant, the 1643 declaration signed by leading Scottish Presbyterians, including

OPPOSITE: *Enzer's coup de théâtre, seen from the gallery.*

TOP: *Arniston illustrated in* Vitruvius Scoticus *(1812), showing the house before the addition of a Victorian porch. The volume, featuring many of Adam's works, is in the library at Arniston.*

ABOVE: *Arniston in its Arcadian setting by Scottish painter Alexander Nasmith (1758–1840).*

OVERLEAF: *Original library in the eaves of the house; the carving and stuccowork are by Josef Enzer. In the nineteenth century the books were moved to the new library on the ground floor.*

ABOVE: *Family sitting room.*

OPPOSITE: *One of the most limpid hangs of Scottish portraiture in existence. The couple playing chess are General and Mrs. Francis Dundas by Henry Raeburn.*

OVERLEAF: *The Oak Room, where the lord president liked to carouse with his cronies.*

Robert Dundas's grandfather, to guarantee the supremacy of Reformed religion. A chip off the old block, Dundas was so low church that he presided over the Court of Session on Christmas Day. However, when it came to architecture, he, like all enlightened Scots equipped with a tolerant eye and clear intellect, saw no conflict in enjoying the Italianate splendor of his baroque house.

Adam razed the old tower house to ground level, retaining two rooms on the south front. Knocking them into one, he paneled the walls in seventeenth-century style with projecting moldings and carved pilasters. This hospitable chamber, known as the Oak Room, was the setting for many a drinking session with the lord president and his cronies, who sat out on the veranda with hogsheads of claret "getting slockened" while admiring the vista, also designed by Adam, which culminated in a cascade.

Despite membership in the ruling elite, Dundas and his peers were slow to cast off traditional Scottish manners and speech. His son, who followed in his father's footsteps to become lord president, once dismayed biographer and diarist James Boswell, whose father was also a judge, by inquiring: "Hoo's yer faither the day, Jamie?"

There was only one drawback to the lord president's satisfaction with his new house. In 1732 building work ground to a halt, leaving, in the words of the family chronicle, "a great muckle hole" where the western third of the main block ought to have stood. Robert Dundas's dreams had run ahead of his purse. On his death in 1753, his heir, the third Robert Dundas, considered selling the place owing to lack of funds. His wife, Henrietta Baillie, would have none of it and sold her own estates in Lanarkshire, enabling him to complete the house.

HENRIETTA BAILLIE
of LAMMINGTON. wife
of LORD PRESIDENT
obit 1755.

By this time, architect William Adam had died; he left his flourishing practice in the hands of his sons John, Robert, and James, however, who went on to achieve national celebrity as the Adam brothers. The eldest, John, took over the completion of Arniston, respecting his father's original exterior design but reconfiguring the interior proportions—heightening the dining and drawing rooms in the newly finished part of the house and putting in a new staircase. Furniture was acquired from William Mathie, a fashionable rococo cabinetmaker in Edinburgh, and Old Masters were procured through brother Robert, who was on his Grand Tour in Italy.

Later generations of Dundases tinkered with the building. An antiquarian raised a pediment on the south front to accommodate the Royal Arms of Scotland salvaged from the Old Parliament building in Edinburgh; he also added a portico to the south front, covering the first lord president's veranda, and his grandson added another to the north entrance to shelter the great hall from the icy blasts of the "Scotch winter."

By the Victorian era, the Dundases had lost all connection with the law. The heir of the day, the sixth Robert Dundas, inherited the estate in 1838 and lived on until 1909. Coal mining on the estate and banking activities in Edinburgh supported his life of philanthropy and local politics, for which he was awarded a baronetcy. He was also a bibliophile and created a new library on the ground floor, preserving Adam's original at the top of the house.

Sir Robert Dundas's unmarried granddaughter, May Dundas, was granted a life tenancy following the early death of her father and lived on quietly in the house until her death in 1970, ending a span of occupation between her and her grandfather of 132 years. This long slumber accounts for the untouched atmosphere of the house, as though it had been trapped in amber. It is also due to its guardianship by May Dundas's heir, Althea Dundas-Bekker, and her daughter Henrietta, who continue to preserve the fabric, contents, and character of this wonderful testament to Scottish genius.

Foulis Castle

ROSS AND CROMARTY

Captain Patrick Munro, who revived clan gatherings at Foulis Castle after World War II, referred to the castle and estate as "the home of all Munros," encouraging members of the far-flung Munro diaspora to visit their clan's seat and birthplace. . . . "The house was always filled with Munros," Hector recalls. "Many came from Canada and the United States, proud of their ancient Scottish roots, and contributed to the restoration of the castle."

Tradition has it that Foulis has been the seat of the Munros for a thousand years, that the clan first staked their claim in AD 1030, when Donald, son of Occan, Prince of Fermanagh, came over from Ireland to assist Malcolm II of Scotland in ridding his kingdom of the Danes. As origin myths go, this one has the ring of authenticity; to this day the lands around Foulis, which are in the highland county of Ross and Cromarty, are referred to as Ferindonald—Donald's land—and early Scottish charters are peppered with references to the Munros serving the monarchs of the Canmore dynasty. Tradition also has it that the clan chief's right of tenure depended upon his gift of a ball of snow from Ben Wyvis, originally part of the estate, whenever so desired by their king. This tradition, as we shall see, was still respected in the eighteenth century.

Hard evidence of the Munros' ancient and continuous ownership of Foulis turned up in 1933 in a deed box marked "last examined in 1826," which contained legal writs stretching back to the early fourteenth century. The current chief, Hector Munro, is the thirty-fourth in a line that can be traced back to 1333.

His father, Captain Patrick Munro, who revived clan gatherings at Foulis Castle after World War II, referred to the castle and estate

as "the home of all Munros," encouraging members of the far-flung Munro diaspora to visit their clan's seat and birthplace. Long settled in North America, the clan can claim the fifth U.S. president, James Monroe, as one of their number. "The house was always filled with Munros," Hector recalls. "Many came from Canada and the United States, proud of their ancient Scottish roots, and contributed to the restoration of the castle."

Such support was essential, as little had been done to the castle for almost a century when Pat Munro (as he was known) and his indomitable wife, Timmy, granddaughter of an Irish peer, inherited the house in 1976. The previous occupant, Pat's mother, who was the clan chief until 1937, when she relinquished it in favor of her son, had been living in the house since 1947, but had taken a dim of view of modernization. "My mother-in-law hated change," Timmy explained.

PRECEDING PAGES: *Distant view of Foulis, described by a visitor in the eighteenth century as "quite Elysian, a most charming site . . . and may truly be termed a Princely Seat."*

OPPOSITE: *One of a pair of nineteenth-century eagle gate piers at the entrance to the castle, indicating its status as the headquarters of a chief. The Scottish Gaelic name for Foulis means "castle gaunt-peaked, the eagle's nest."*

ABOVE: *The Great Seal of James VI of Scotland & I of England, dated 1615, one of many such documents in the muniment room.*

ABOVE: *The courtyard is flanked by outbuildings that originally housed services such as the laundry, dairy, and bakehouse.*

RIGHT: *Late-fifteenth-century "keyhole" gun loop, uncovered in a courtyard storeroom wall.*

BELOW: *Hector Munro's highland bonnet, sporting his chief's eagle feathers.*

OPPOSITE: *The asymmetrical courtyard elevation. The longer, west (right-hand) wing was rebuilt in 1750–54 as a ballroom after the Jacobite burning.*

"The house had no electric lights; there were twenty bedrooms and one bathroom, which had been put in in 1891. Even when electricity was installed, she went on using gas lamps for a year afterwards." Hector Munro remembers climbing up to "granny's" attics as a boy to place buckets under the holes in the roof. "There were so many, it was like a sieve." The roof was repaired in 1958, thanks to a Historic Buildings Council grant, the first to be awarded to a house in Ross-shire.

In the fifteenth century the Scottish Gaelic name of Foulis Castle was, roughly translated, "castle gaunt-peaked, the eagle's nest," reflecting its status as headquarters of the chief. Today, though the chief still has the right to wear three eagle feathers in his bonnet, as highlanders' headgear is known, his castle's appearance is a mellow congregation of buildings: an expansive Georgian mansion overlooking in one direction the Cromarty Firth and in the other an oblong courtyard flanked by service buildings that once housed the laundry, stables, dairy, and bakehouse. A tower still projects from the north front and soars above the courtyard, but like the rest of the building, it is wrapped in an elegant Georgian façade of sash windows and weather-beaten harling, a stone-based

rendering used in Scotland to shield buildings from the elements. Only during the restorations in the 1970s and 1980s were the castle's massive foundation walls revealed, indicating its early defensive purpose. Further evidence of fortifications in the shape of four "keyhole" gun loops came to light when the masonry of a storeroom in the courtyard was uncovered.

The Georgian rebuilding of Foulis Castle followed its partial destruction by a Jacobite force during the 1745 Rebellion. Like a number of highland clans, the Munros were staunch supporters of the government forces, which stemmed from their fierce Presbyterianism, as expressed in the family's motto, "Dread God." According to family lore, the Munros pledged their allegiance to the Hanoverian cause in time-honored fashion by delivering a basket of snow from Ben Wyvis to the Duke of Cumberland. The family paid for their loyalty. The chief, Sir Robert Munro, and his brother Dr. Duncan Munro were killed at the Battle of Falkirk, fighting

Charles Stutfield 71st Highlanders.
George Munro 42d Highlanders.

the Jacobite rebels to the last as the English soldiers under Sir Robert's command fled.

Following the government victory at Culloden, the heir to Foulis, the twenty-seventh chief, Sir Harry Munro, set about rebuilding his house, paid for with government compensation. A high-ceilinged ballroom (now the drawing room) was thrown up on the site of the west wing, which had been burned down, but extended in length so that the tower was no longer centered on the courtyard elevation. This imbalance on what was then the entrance front suggests the hand of a dilettante on a budget. Sir Harry himself, who was described

by the architect Robert Adam, no less, as "a well known scholar and classic," may have been responsible, albeit with the support of a master builder; his eye for classical detail and proportion undoubtedly contributed to the clever harmonization between the old and new portions of the house despite its uneven plan. The master builder is thought to have been a man named Boag who worked for several lairds in the locality.

Sir Harry's restorations met with high praise from a visiting bishop in August 1762 on a tour of his highland see. "Foulis Castle," wrote Bishop Forbes, "is quite Elysian, a most charming site, decorated with finished Policies and may truly be termed a Princely Seat."

A few elegant flourishes were added by the next chief, Sir Hugh. To the main entrance, which his predecessor had moved to the south front, he added a double flight of steps with smart iron railings and lamps worthy of a town house in London (where Sir Hugh had spent much of his life), leading to a new classical doorway.

RIGHT: *Sweeping view of Foulis's barley fields with the Cromarty Firth in the distance.*

BELOW: *Victorian chief Sir Hector Munro sharing a glass or two with a friend.*

OPPOSITE: *Curling, like golf, was invented by the Scots. A row of 1890s Victorian stones in their original panniers at Foulis (top). An 1897 curling match with a fine array of beards, moustaches, and bonnets (bottom).*

OVERLEAF LEFT: *A basket-hilted broadsword and an assortment of Munro tartans showing variations in color.*

OVERLEAF RIGHT: *The 31st chief, Sir Hector Munro, who moved back into the house with his wife, Violet, beginning its rehabilitation.*

PAGES 106–7: *The eighteenth-century kitchen with its original table.*

PAGES 108–9: *Augustan and Victorian personalities recorded at Foulis.*

In 1803 tragedy struck. Sir Hugh's young wife was drowned swimming in the Cromarty Firth. Her death led to years of feuding between the grieving widower and his heir, a much-hated distant cousin. All the furniture was sold or destroyed, the woods felled, and the estate mortgaged. The Munros effectively abandoned their castle for the nearby dower house until 1890, when the young Victorian heir Hector Munro, who became chief and baronet four years later, and his wife, Violet Stirling, whose father had made a fortune in mining during the Industrial Revolution, moved back into Foulis.

The castle's long rehabilitation had begun. Since then four generations, including the present chief, Hector, and his son, Finian, have dedicated their lives to securing the estate. Whenever possible, original furniture, portraits, and armorial china have been bought back to add to the furnishings acquired at the turn of the twentieth century. The mixed estate of woodland and arable land is farmed by Hector with such success that he has bought back 1,400 acres that had to be sold after the war. He has also created a clan center in the old family storehouse on the Cromarty Firth, which will provide an added source of income in years to come. From the top of the tower there is a dazzling view over the firth. In the fields below, his barley sways in the breeze. "My wife, Alpha," he says, "plays the fiddle and often strikes up 'The Wind That Shakes the Barley'"—an apt celebration of the remarkable survival of the Clan Munro and their thousand-year tenure of Foulis.

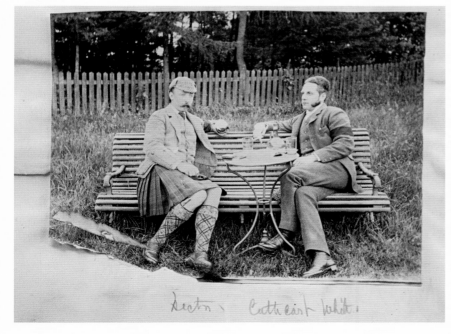

HOT
WATER

TOWER ROOM   BATH ROOM   BED ROOM
Nº I.

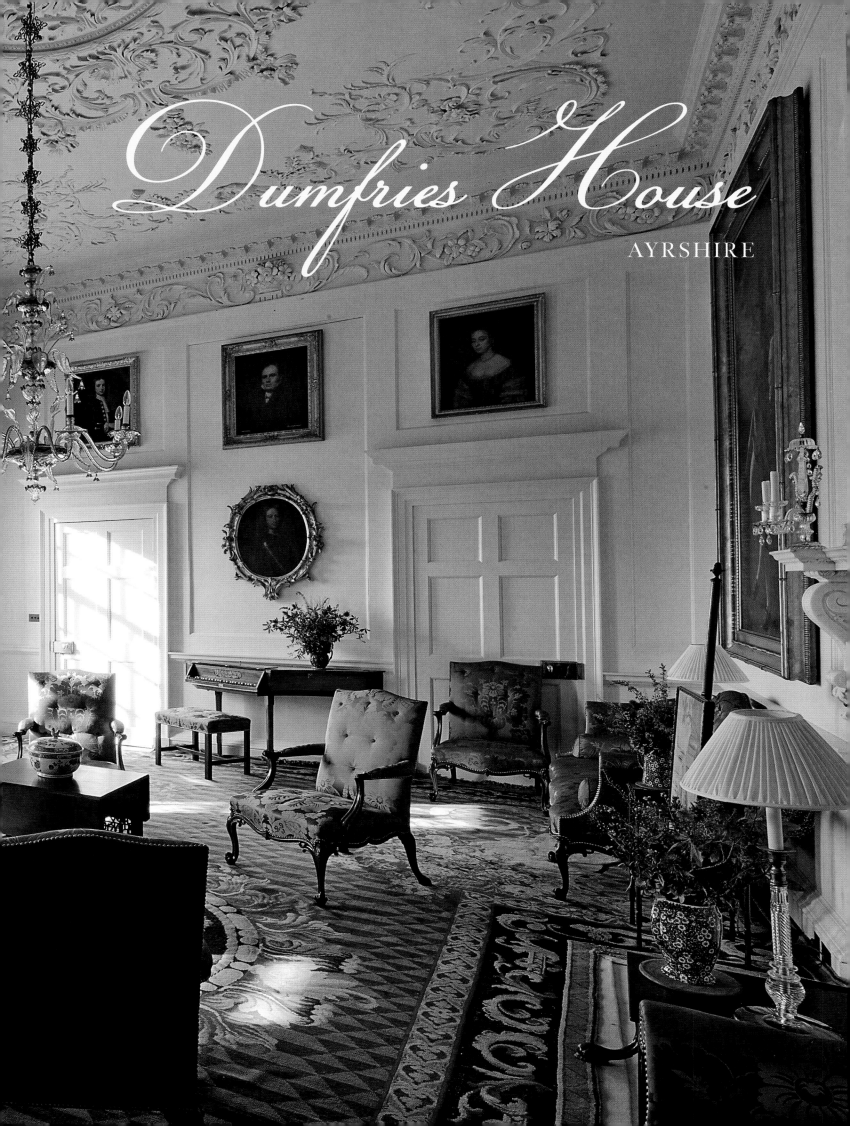

Dumfries House

AYRSHIRE

The grace of the exterior is matched by the "lightness" of the interior décor, to use the Adams' own word for the rococo-style ceilings, overdoors, and picture frames, which run wild with foliage and flowers, pomegranates and peaches, scrolls, cartouches, and masks—all created in anticipation of Lord Dumfries's purchase of fashionable new furnishings.

The story of Dumfries House can be summed up in two invitations. The first, on May 26, 1760, was from the fifth Earl of Dumfries to Lord Bute, inviting him to celebrate the Prince of Wales's birthday on June 4 at his newly completed Dumfries House in Ayrshire. The second, in June 2007, was from the Prince of Wales's office in Clarence House to campaigners and private and government benefactors who had supported him in the last-minute rescue of Dumfries House for the nation. The party given by the Prince on July 12, 2007, took place 247 years after Lord Dumfries celebrated his ancestor's birthday—a most timely return of the compliment.

The host of the first party, the fifth Earl of Dumfries, was a distinguished career soldier who had retired in 1747 to his ancestral estate in Ayrshire. Plans were soon afoot to replace the sixteenth-century "mansion place," known as Leifnorris, with a classical house designed by renowned architect William Adam's sons John and Robert, with advice supplied by arbiter of taste Lord Hopetoun, himself a patron of the Adam brothers. Discussions dragged on for six years with debate over design and cost. Agreement was finally reached in 1754 to build a three-story block consisting of

"Rustick basement," "Principal Story," and "Attick," along with "Collonades in the form of Clos [closed] Arcades" and "Two Pavilions."

The earl (who evidently loved any excuse for a party) laid the foundation stone on July 18, 1754, with much music, dancing, and toasting of health. In attendance was twenty-six-year-old Robert Adam, who reported that he had found the earl "in good health and top humour . . . we are always merry and laughing."

PRECEDING PAGES: *The blue drawing room is appointed with an Axminster carpet (1755), William Mathie gilt-wood mirrors (1759), George Mercer console tables, and a Thomas Chippendale suite of elbow chairs and settees (1759), newly uphol-stered in silk damask from a pattern found in the house.*

OPPOSITE: *Recently restored decoration in the pewter corridor, part of Scottish architect Robert Weir Schultz's discreet enlargement of the flanking pavilions in the 1890s.*

ABOVE: *William, fifth Earl of Dumfries, builder of the house, by Thomas Hudson, 1759.*

ABOVE: *The Dumfries coat of arms resting on a nest of thistles ornaments the pediment of the entrance front.*

BELOW: *The design of the fruit and vegetable swag in the pink dining room is attributed to Robert Adam.*

OPPOSITE: *Rococo festivity, starring an eighteenth-century Murano chandelier.*

OVERLEAF: *Entrance hall. The plasterwork was colored and gilded in 1877.*

He had good reason to be happy. The Adam brothers had designed a beautiful, pared-down, classical house, an essay in pure architecture reliant solely on scale and proportion for effect. Constructed from rose-tinted sandstone quarried on the estate, its only embellishment is a crisply carved pediment replete with coats of arms resting on a bed of Scottish thistles, emblematic of the Knighthood of the Thistle conferred on the earl by George II. The self-confidence of the Adams' work, deemed their greatest early country house, is a harbinger of masterpieces to come.

The grace of the exterior is matched by the "lightness" of the interior décor, to use the Adams' own word for the rococo-style ceilings, overdoors, and picture frames, which run wild with foliage and flowers, pomegranates and peaches, scrolls, cartouches, and masks—all created in anticipation of Lord Dumfries's purchase of fashionable new furnishings. Long before completion, Robert Adam was reporting from London that he had seen "a thousand things every day that would answer charmingly for your habitation and that would tempt a Saint." The earl was easily seduced, having been a habitué of the cabinetmakers' workshops in Edinburgh that supplied furniture to old Leifnorris House, and went shopping on an epic scale. He ordered quantities of furniture from the city's greatest cabinetmakers—Alexander Peter, Francis Brodie, and William Mathie; from Alexander Peter alone, just under one hundred "seats," eight four-posters, and a

variety of tables and other items. His spree continued in London, where he purchased over fifty items from Thomas Chippendale's workshop, including some of his finest pieces, many illustrated in his famous trade catalogue, *The Gentleman and Cabinet-Maker's Director*, such as the parcel-gilt state bed, hung with blue damask, and the parcel-gilt padouk and gilded-limewood breakfront bookcase. All were shipped to the port of Leith, thence by cart to Ayrshire. Aware of Scotland's weather, Chippendale explained to Lord Dumfries, "... we have packed the Damk [damask] furniture in glew'd case to prevent any damage by Water we would beg your Lordship to order the Carriages to have such covering as will turn rain lest they show'd meet it upon the Road."

Every invoice and instruction concerning Dumfries House has been preserved, making the collection of unique value, particularly the Scottish furniture, which rarely has any surviving documentation to identify the maker.

It's no wonder Lord Dumfries threw a party right after moving into his dazzling new house in 1760. But he also had another motive. A childless widower, just turned sixty, he had his eye on one of the guests, Lady Mary Douglas. He did remarry but died childless in 1768 at Dumfries House.

His title, house, and estate passed to a nephew, whose daughter Lady Elizabeth Crichton married John Viscount Mount Stuart, eldest son of the Marquess of Bute. Both died tragically young, but not before producing an heir, who ultimately inherited the Bute and Dumfries titles. The passing of the house into Bute ownership brought to an end its brief period as a principal family seat. The Bute guardianship, however, saved it. The second Marquess of Bute became one of the most brilliant industrialists of the Victorian age, turning his ancient landed family into one of the richest in the British Empire. Much of their fortune was spent indulging their passion for architecture—building, restoring, remodeling, and in the case of Dumfries House, conserving. The only intervention was the doubling in size of the flanking pavilions, executed with such discretion that it is hardly noticeable.

Although house and contents were excellently maintained, no family member lived there for any length of time from the early 1800s until 1934, when John Dumfries, the future fifth marquess and his bride, Lady Eileen Forbes, took up residence. Eileen Bute was a daughter of the Irish peer Lord Granard and his American wife, Beatrice Mills, daughter of a keen race horse owner and breeder from Dutchess County, New York. The house was requisitioned during the war and afterward remained unoccupied until 1956, when the recently widowed Lady Eileen moved back in.

Writer and photographer Christopher Simon Sykes has described Eileen Bute as "a forceful gregarious woman, a horse racing enthusiast who loved a stiff vodka and had a voice husky from chain smoking Embassy cigarettes. She lived in the white drawing room, whose walls and ceiling were stained yellow from the nicotine generated by her and a small group of fellow widows, nicknamed the Ayrshire Widows Association." He could have added the circle of old gentlemen in attendance, known as the Dowager Colonels, who had served in the Ayrshire Yeomanry during the war.

Her grandson John Bute, the seventh Marquess of Bute, remembers his grandmother with great affection. "She had a stoical side," he says. "Whatever life threw at her, she would deal with it. Her husband, my grandfather, died at forty-seven, which meant she had a long widowhood—and had to start her life again in Ayrshire."

As a small child, John Bute used to visit his grandmother from the family's principal seat, Mount Stuart, on the Isle of Bute, in the company of the head gardener, Jock McVey, who was dispatched to check up on the Dumfries House gardens. "I used to hang out with Jock, who was quite a fearsome character—putting up with no nonsense—but he and my grandmother had a fantastic relationship."

John Bute sums up his memories of the last member of his family to live at Dumfries House: "She was a stunning-looking woman with huge energy, always surrounded by people. To me personally, Grandma offered unconditional love."

Eileen Bute died in 1993, having lived in the house longer than any member of the family since it was built. Her son, the sixth marquess, and a great benefactor of heritage causes in Scotland, died that same year. His heir, the current John Bute, reluctantly chose to sell Dumfries House to protect the long-term future of his family and their principal seat, Mount Stuart. His decision triggered the campaign led by the Prince of Wales—as recounted in the Introduction—that opened a dynamic new phase in the house's history.

Bowhill

SELKIRKSHIRE

"*W*alter Scott," says Richard Buccleuch, "was also half in love with the duke's wife, Harriet, who was his muse. She inspired him to write the Lay of the Last Minstrel, where he speaks of 'Sweet Bowhill.'"

The doorbell at Bowhill is an intercom bearing a small, worn, white sticker inscribed "Their Graces" in ballpoint pen. The informality combined with grandeur sums up this house, one of the two principal seats of the Duke and Duchess of Buccleuch and Queensberry in Scotland, the other being Drumlanrig (see pages 51–69). "This has not always been the case, as until 1914 Dalkeith Palace took precedence," says Richard Buccleuch, the tenth duke, who inherited from his father in 2007. "Bowhill was a huge but simple retreat for country pleasures, with none of the treasures now on view, just scores of paintings of favourite horses, hounds, and dogs and dark classical landscapes by the clerical amateur, the Rev John Thomson." The status of Bowhill changed after World War I, when Montagu House in London was given up and Dalkeith Palace in Midlothian was not reopened for family use.

Situated some thirty miles southeast of Dalkeith, Bowhill was a natural place to retrench, as it was more accessible to the great landholdings of the Scotts of Buccleuch, which had been built up since the thirteenth century and today extend over forty-six thousand acres of wild country running southwest from Selkirk and Hawick to the English border.

Originally a plain Queen Anne box with low wings, the house, set in "a pretty little estate," had been acquired by the Buccleuchs in 1745 but had remained largely overlooked by the family until 1812, when the fourth duke, a keen shot, commissioned the architect William Stark to add a neat Regency villa onto the south front of the existing building. Stark's simple classical design, realized in gray whinstone, set the style for all future additions to the house, regardless of the architects' natural preference. On Stark's death in 1813, William Atkinson, better known for his Gothic work, continued Stark's campaign of enlargement, adding a suite of reception rooms and family quarters over the next six years. "I think

PRECEDING PAGES: *Entrance front created by William Burn in 1832.*

OPPOSITE: *Scrolls, books, and busts clutter the archivist's lair.*

ABOVE: *Hunting scenes and portraits—souvenirs of Bowhill as a sporting retreat—in the inner hall.*

OVERLEAF LEFT: *Sir Joshua Reynolds's Winter, a portrait of Caroline Scott, 1777, in the dining room.*

OVERLEAF RIGHT: *Louis XV chairs and writing table and a Boulle bracket clock lend a French flavor to the saloon. The portrait is by studio of van Dyck.*

this addition will add much to our comfort and convenience," wrote Duke Charles to his close friend and kinsman, the author Walter Scott. "It gives *me* a bedroom, dressing room (which I shall use as a depository for guns and fishing tackle), a sitting room and a servants' room, all connecting. The sitting room connects with the library by a sham book door."

Duke and Poet were intimate friends, sharing a love of books and the Border country, as well as the same architect in Atkinson, who was also assisting Scott at Abbotsford, which is only eight miles from Bowhill. "Scott," says Richard Buccleuch, "was also half in love with the duke's wife,

Harriet, who was his muse. She inspired him to write the *Lay of the Last Minstrel*, where he speaks of 'Sweet Bowhill.'" In return, Scott acted as mentor to Duke Charles and his eldest son, Walter, to whom he was guardian.

"Scott was for them such a role model," explains Richard Buccleuch. "He had huge sensitivity towards the rural population and the rural economy—and wrote directly to the fourth and fifth dukes about their responsibilities. His early life was spent recreating the minstrelsy—roaming the Borders, writing down the oral stories. He had this ability to relate to people across the social spectrum: a complete mixer. He was fascinated in every aspect of an estate, such as not just planting trees but their provenance. That sort of stewardship was what he thought the young fourth and fifth dukes should practice."

His spirit lives on today. "I just think Sir Walter Scott was an all round good egg," Richard Buccleuch says, "with all the sort of instincts one would like." As a result, the library at Bowhill is no shrine to dead authors but stacked with new books, many submitted for the Walter Scott Prize for historical fiction established two years ago by him and his wife, Elizabeth, with the winner announced at the annual Borders Book Festival.

The Victorian fifth duke took Scott's words on stewardship to heart and became a great agricultural improver and industrial developer, who, as one obituarist put it, "went to his office and transacted business much the same as a city merchant would do." All the more reason for turning Bowhill into the ultimate country retreat, which was set in motion in 1832 with the commissioning of Scottish architect William Burn to remodel and enlarge the house. A master planner, Burn was

PRECEDING PAGES: *William Burn's double-height saloon provides the perfect setting for Mortlake tapestries, woven ca. 1670, after Mantegna's* Triumph of Caesar *cycle at Hampton Court Palace.*

RIGHT: *In the jewelbox-like boudoir, a chinoiserie mirror hangs against Chinese wallpaper.*

FAR RIGHT: *Fringes and tassels bedeck needlepoint-covered chairs.*

BELOW: *Boudoir ephemera.*

OPPOSITE: *The boudoir is a frenzy of needlepoint and rococo revival.*

OVERLEAF: *The drawing room, with its crimson damask–covered walls.*

PAGES 146–47: *Burn extended the house to accommodate a larger dining room.*

attuned to every requirement of his grand Victorian clients with their crowd of children (the Buccleuchs had seven) and army of servants, mapping out country houses along rational lines. At Bowhill, he moved the entrance to the north front, which now opens onto a parade of outer and inner halls, culminating in the towering saloon, a place to get one's bearings before heading off east or west down the service corridor that runs along the spine of house.

Burn retained the comfortable reception rooms at the core of the old Regency house, although an enlarged drawing room was dignified with rich crimson damask. But he extended the house to incorporate a larger dining room and a family apartment with the duchess's boudoir at its heart, a glittering casket of a room, lined with old Chinese wallpaper and laden with silks, fringes, and needlepoint in an exquisite fusion of form and purpose.

Like many functionalists, Burn's strength lay in the fine tuning of his "machine for living," to retrofit Le Corbusier's famous dictum, rather than in creating a pleasing exterior. His new entrance front at Bowhill absorbed the surviving fragment of the Queen Anne house and extended Stark and Atkinson's villa in an elongated stretch of gray whinstone. This suited his client, who, according to the current duke, "wasn't building to impress anyone. It had to be practical." Even so, Burn's attempt at adding a picturesque feature to yet another extension in 1870 led the duchess to remark of his clock tower, "Burn should pay us to take it down."

The twentieth century saw one last transformation of Bowhill. "In 1910, when the picture catalogue was done," says Richard Buccleuch, "there was nothing in the way of art—and there are no photographs of pre-1920 interiors, as the house didn't merit it." All this was soon

to change with the arrival of treasures from Montagu House and Dalkeith Palace, a stream of French marquetry furniture, including many pieces with royal provenance; British portraiture by Reynolds, Gainsborough, Lawrence, and their peers; Mortlake tapestries after Mantegna; and Claude Lorrains and other Old Masters, not to mention troves of silver, miniatures, and Sèvres porcelain. Belying its plain exterior, the well-planned house with its varying scales of rooms—from the double-height saloon, tailor made for the Mortlake tapestries, to the broad dining room, well lit for portraits—provided the perfect setting for the collection.

Not only did the Buccleuchs themselves collect, but they also acquired great collections through marriage, notably that of the dukes of Montagu, the last of whose line, Elizabeth Montagu, was the wife of the cultivated third duke. Also brought to Bowhill were the relics of the Buccleuchs' royal ancestor the Duke of Monmouth, illegitimate son of Charles II, who married Scott heiress the Countess of Buccleuch. Their marriage in 1663 signaled the creation of the Dukedom of Buccleuch. Following her husband's execution after the Monmouth rebellion, Anne Duchess of Buccleuch was made duchess in her own right to protect her estates from confiscation, and she lived out her long life at Dalkeith Palace. Her portrait now hangs at Bowhill in the library above the chimneypiece (also from Dalkeith), which is carved with her initials, a reminder that the family's "simple retreat" has also become the store of collective memory for the Buccleuch family.

"Bowhill," says Richard Buccleuch, "reminds us of the need to remain rooted."

Ballindalloch Castle

BANFFSHIRE

ANSE ET ANIMO

TOUCH NOT THE CAT BOT A GLOVE

YE LORD SHALL PRESERVE THY GOING OUT & THY COMING IN

"*W*hen I took over," recalls Clare, "I spent a great deal of time rummaging in the attic. My dear papa said, 'There are some ghastly paintings up there, but before putting them on the bonfire you might just show them to the experts from the auction houses.'" . . . Now on display throughout the house, they represent the most important collection of seventeenth-century Spanish paintings in private hands in Scotland."*

"Ask the owner of any great house and they will tell you that inheriting is the easy part," says Clare Macpherson-Grant Russell, lady laird of Ballindalloch Castle. "It's hanging onto the place that's hard." Her family have succeeded in doing so since 1546, although there have been rocky moments along the way, not least the problem of the fifth baronet, "naughty Uncle George," who left the bulk of his will in 1950 to his boyfriend. "He was really very modern for his day," says Clare. All the Macpherson ancestral lands, totaling over 150,000 acres, had to be sold. However, the decision by her father, Sir Ewan Macpherson-Grant, to keep the original Grant estate, which extends to 25,000 acres along the valley of the Spey, with its prime farmland in Banffshire, has proved a sound one. Her parents moved in in 1952, knocked down a Victorian wing, rewired, plumbed, added four new bathrooms (previously there was one), and moved the kitchen "a quarter of a mile" from the basement to the same floor as the dining room. Their vital contribution was the start of the revival of Ballindalloch.

When Clare and her husband, Oliver Russell, took over the running of the castle and estate from her father in 1978, there were still thirty people working

solely for the family, including keepers, ghillies, and parlormaids. "In those days," explained Clare, "you just lived like a laird." Oliver Russell, who springs from a line of distinguished diplomats and public servants, had been a banker before moving north. From the start, he and Clare worked together on planning the long-term survival of the estate. "He looks at the overall picture and develops the strategy," says Clare, "and I put it into practice and take care of the minutiae." Their partnership has worked brilliantly, even though, as Clare admits, "we have

PRECEDING PAGES: *Entrance front of Ballindalloch, showing the original sixteenth-century tower house and one of the Georgian wings to the right, all with Victorian detailing.*

OPPOSITE: *Coat of arms of the Macpherson-Grants above the front door, installed as part of the 1850 alterations. The Macpherson motto, "Touch not the cat bot a glove," alludes to the clan's fiery nature.*

LEFT: *Sir George Macpherson-Grant, fifth Baronet of Ballindalloch (1890–1950), known as "naughty Uncle George." Painted by David Jagger.*

RIGHT: *Portrait of General James Grant as a boy by Richard Waitt, family painter of the Clan Grant. The boy fulfilled his military ambition fighting in North America. He also made the Georgian additions to Ballindalloch.*

BELOW: *George Washington's letter to General James Grant concerning the safe delivery of supplies and money to British and German prisoners after the battles of Trenton and Princeton.*

OPPOSITE: *Classic Scottish crowstepping over the archway into the courtyard.*

OVERLEAF: *Ingenious vaulting of the new hall in the old tower house, created in 1850 by architect Thomas MacKenzie.*

been tackling the challenge of modernising a traditional highland estate ever since."

Dating from 1546, Ballindalloch is a classic example of a fortified tower house that has grown gracefully over the years to reflect the need in more settled times for comfort rather than defense, though the first phase of expansion, ironically, was paid for by the dividends of war. In 1770 the 12th laird, General James Grant, soldier, entrepreneur, and epicure, added a pair of elegant wings to north and south, one to accommodate a drawing room, library, and smoking room and the other his chef, a French-speaking emancipated slave from America. The general had done well out there fighting the French and the Cherokee Indians in the French and Indian War. His success was rewarded

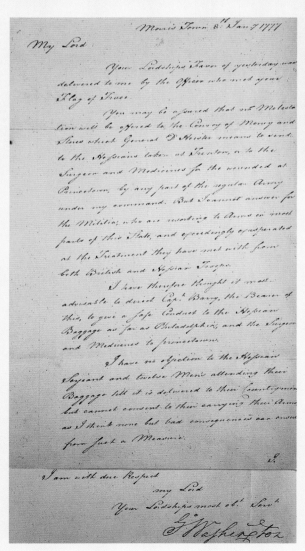

with the governorship of Florida, where he developed his own highly profitable plantations of rice and indigo. He went on to fight in the American War of Independence, taking part in the battles of New York and Trenton; among his important American papers, still held by the family, is a letter to him from George Washington concerning the victualing of Revolutionary War prisoners.

General James, who died without issue, left Ballindalloch to his nephew George Macpherson, chieftain of one of the most important septs, or branches, of the famous clan established at Invereshie and owner of its vast estates. His inheritance united the two clans of the Strathspey valley,

154

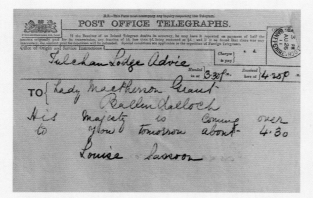

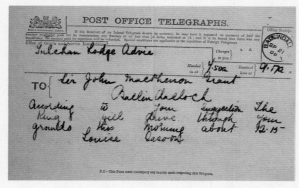

which was recognized in the creation of his baronetcy in 1838, when he styled himself Sir George Macpherson-Grant of Ballindalloch and Invereshie. The title was to die out with Clare Russell's father.

In 1850 the second baronet, Sir John, made the greatest changes to the house, employing an accomplished local architect and scholar of Scottish Baronial style, Thomas MacKenzie, who spruced up the decorative features of the tower house and Georgian wings and added a sympathetic courtyard block. The library and dining room were fitted out with handsome paneling, and a new entrance hall was created in the tower house, a beautifully plastered vaulted space springing from a central pillar. Most of his work, both inside and out, is remarkable for its restraint, which brings out the character—both forbidding and easeful—of this classic Scottish country house.

Sir John Macpherson-Grant's other legacy was only rediscovered when the Russells moved in. "When I took over," recalls Clare, "I spent a great deal of time rummaging in the attic. My dear papa said, 'There are

some ghastly paintings up there, but before putting them on the bonfire you might just show them to the experts from the auction houses.'" These turned out to be a collection of Spanish paintings, including works by Ribera, Zurbarán, and Meléndez, acquired by Sir John when serving in the 1840s as secretary in the British legation in Lisbon. Now on display throughout the house, they represent the most important collection of seventeenth-century Spanish paintings in private hands in Scotland and are one of the earliest collections in Britain to have been brought from Spain.

Being shown around Ballindalloch by the lady laird is akin to taking a walk with royalty. One emerges from the family wing, originally built by General James for his chef, into a corridor that is hung floor to ceiling with photographs of the Russells and their children and grandchildren, who represent the twenty-third and twenty-fourth generations of the Grant family at Ballindalloch. Clare Russell is also pictured in her role as lord lieutenant for Banffshire, the Queen's representative in the county. Links with the royal family are strong: Oliver Russell's father was second sea lord and aide-de-camp to the Queen, their son Guy was also a page of honour to the Queen, and the Queen Mother was a frequent visitor to Ballindalloch from her own Castle of Mey. The corridor is crammed with visitors engrossed in the photographs, revealing the importance of maintaining a family's presence in a historic house. "Welcome," she says. "This is first and foremost a family home, as you'll see from all our photographs." Visitors gather round as the lady laird introduces herself. "You're all the way from Germany? Wine growers? We make whisky."

Ballindalloch's links with the whisky industry stretch back to the 1745 Rebellion,

when the laird of the day, despite supporting the Hanoverian cause, gave refuge to a fleeing Jacobite, Alexander Grant, after the Battle of Culloden. The fugitive's descendant went on to found the famous firm of William Grant & Sons, which built the first distillery on the river Spey—Glenfiddich— just up the valley from Ballindalloch. The Macpherson-Grants had their own distillery for a time, founded by the Victorian laird Sir George Macpherson-Grant, who promoted the industry through investing in the railways, facilitating the transport of whisky to bonded warehouses; the station at Ballindalloch was opened in 1863.

This innovative Victorian laird also proved outstanding in animal husbandry, particularly in creating and perfecting the Aberdeen Angus breed, which he and two other landowners bred from the native strains of black cattle found in the northeast of Scotland. His Ballindalloch herd, founded in 1860, which still grazes peacefully in the meadows around the castle, is the oldest in the world and every Aberdeen Angus steak eaten today derives from this famous bloodline. His achievement is recorded in the portraits of his prize-winning cows and bulls by Scottish artist David George Steell, and celebrated in his silver trophies.

Farming is just one of the income streams that have been developed by Oliver and Clare Russell since they began running the estate some thirty-four years ago. Others are tourism, corporate entertaining, and sport. Fishing on its famous beats on the river Spey, stalking on its deer forests, and shooting on its moors all contribute to the survival of this great Highland estate. Never satisfied, Oliver Russell was asked a decade or so back by Clare what he would like for his birthday. "A golf course," came the reply, and she duly built one as another commercial activity on the estate.

The lady laird is also the author of a best-selling cookbook, *I Love Food*, which draws on her early days as "chief cook and bottle washer" for the castle's paying sporting guests and international visitors. Many of the dishes are inspired by produce from the estate, not least the three world-famous ingredients from Speyside—beef, salmon, and whisky. Her recipe for Ballindalloch Aberdeen Angus fillet comes with the tempting instruction for the sauce: "Add whisky to taste."

A key to her book's success is the section devoted to tidbits for dogs entitled "Woof!— Let's not forget the dog!" It typifies the joie de vivre and attention to detail that have made Oliver and Clare Russell's achievement at Ballindalloch such a triumph.

Lochinch Castle

WIGTOWNSHIRE

Even for Scotland, the natural setting is extraordinary. The castle stands on an isthmus between two lochs (lakes): one is named the White Loch of Inch, hence "Lochinch"; the other is called the Black Loch. . . . The new layout, which survives to this day, consisted of tree-lined allées, a canal linking the two lochs, a round pond, and terraces and banks that run down from the castle, forming lookout points over the Black Loch.

Lochinch, an outstanding example of Scottish Baronial architecture, represents a late flowering of the "auld alliance" between France and Scotland, brought about by the marriage in 1846 of John Dalrymple, tenth Earl of Stair, to Louisa de Franquetot, daughter of the third duc de Coigny. Together, they built a new family seat on the ancestral Stair estate, situated in the farthest reaches of southwest Scotland, which the first Viscount Stair had acquired in 1674. The original house, Castle Kennedy, had burned down in 1716, and though the family continued to develop the gardens and estate, their principal residence remained at Newliston, a William Adam house, outside Edinburgh.

As to the Stairs' decision to build Lochinch, the present countess, Emily Stair, says, "We don't know precisely why. Perhaps Louisa, who was socially speaking equal to the Stairs, wanted to establish her own provenance in Scotland." Indeed, hers was one of the most dashing and glamorous of the Ancien Régime. Her ancestor, the first duc de Coigny, proved an outstanding general in the wars waged by Louis XV, ending his days as a Maréchal de France; the second duc also shone on the battlefield, for which he earned the position of first equerry to Louis XVI at Versailles, where he was

a friend of Marie Antoinette. A cousin at court was less reputable. Her antics inspired the character of the marquise de Merteuil in Laclos's tale of sexual manipulation, *Les Liaisons dangereuses*. After the Revolution, de Coigny served the Bourbons in exile acting as a diplomatic envoy, returning to Paris with Louis XVIII in 1815, when he too was made a Maréchal de France. Louisa's father, the third duc, who was grandson of the second (his father having been killed in a duel), fought for Napoleon. During the Russian campaign he lost an arm, which he insisted on carrying in a portmanteau

PRECEDING PAGES: *Scottish Baronial in all its glory, designed by James Wardrop, 1864–68.*

OPPOSITE: *View of the drawing room from the library.*

ABOVE: *Co-builder of the house, John Dalrymple, tenth Earl of Stair, in a portrait by Rudolf Lehmann.*

on the retreat from Moscow until finally abandoning it, to the relief of his soldiers.

Scottish blood also flowed through Louisa's veins. Her mother, Henrietta Dalrymple Hamilton, who married the duc de Coigny in 1822, sprang from a cadet branch of the Stair family and stood to inherit one of the Dalrymple estates, Bargeny in Ayrshire. Her cosmopolitan parents spent much time on the Continent and educated Henrietta in France. Even so, they were dismayed by her marriage to de Coigny, believing that Bargeny would ultimately pass into foreign ownership. However, the duc and duchesse de Coigny habitually spent six months of the year at Bargeny, where their daughter, Louisa, would have met her distant cousin, John Dalrymple, the future Earl of Stair.

Springing from a line of Ayrshire lairds, the Stairs, whose family name is Dalrymple,

soared to prominence in the seventeenth century, thanks to the first viscount, a brilliant lawyer, considered one of the founders of the modern Scottish legal system. Shrewd, principled, and ambitious, he charted a course through the dangerous waters surrounding the fall of the Catholic James II, returning from political exile in 1688 in King William's flagship. The Stairs' position at the Protestant court of William and Mary and their successors was assured. The viscount's son, who was created Earl of Stair, achieved the highest legal and political appointments in Scotland, and the next in line, John Dalrymple, who inherited the earldom in 1707, earned glory on the European stage as a military commander under Marlborough in his string of victories against the French. His subsequent appointment as ambassador to the Court of Versailles burnished his reputation. Both father and son were assiduous in

PRECEDING PAGES: *In the dining room, the second Earl of Stair presides above the fireplace; the battle scene on the adjacent wall celebrates a de Coigny victory.*

RIGHT: *Jacobean revival staircase.*

BELOW: *Queen Elizabeth II inspecting the Royal Company of Archers, the Sovereign's bodyguard in Scotland. Her Captain-General (behind her) bearing his gold stick of office is the 13th Earl of Stair, the present earl's father.*

OPPOSITE: *Portrait of the present earl's aunts above a billiards scoreboard in the inner hall.*

OVERLEAF: *The drawing room.*

protecting the Protestant settlement against Jacobite rebellion, which left the former tainted by association with the order that led to the Massacre of Glencoe. His son, as ambassador to France, thwarted Jacobite ambitions especially at the time of the 1715 rebellion, leading his descendant the present Earl of Stair to speculate that the burning of Castle Kennedy in 1716 was no mere accident: "What if a resentful Jacobite under the guise of a servant at the castle had decided to take revenge?"

The second earl chose not to rebuild the castle but to use the imposing ruin as a focal point in his ambitious plans for a new garden and designed landscape at Castle Kennedy. His knowledge of Louis XIV's vast formal gardens and park at Versailles informed the scale and ambition of the project, which was commissioned from Scottish landscape designer William Boutcher in 1722, just two years after the earl's recall from France. Even for Scotland, the natural setting is extraordinary. The castle stands on an isthmus between two lochs (lakes): one is named the White Loch of Inch, hence "Lochinch"; the other is called the Black Loch, or Loch Crindel, and boasts a man-made island dating back to the Bronze Age. The new layout, which survives to this day, consisted of tree-lined allées, a canal linking the two lochs, a round pond, and terraces and banks that run down from the castle, forming lookout points over the Black Loch. Work continued until the earl's death in 1747, after which the gardens were virtually abandoned for more than a hundred years until John and Louisa Stair decided to build their romantic new house on the shore of the White Loch, directly aligned with Castle Kennedy.

Commissioned from the well-connected architect James Wardrop, a kinsman of the

Stairs, work commenced in 1864, the year of John Dalrymple's accession to the earldom. "I have great admiration for the way the house was built," says the present earl, Jamie Stair, "without cranes and with everything having to be cut and fitted on site. Growing up here in a house this size—how do you compare it? Large scale was the normality."

Lochinch is the ultimate Scottish Baronial house—a massing of ranges and wings, as tall and deep as they are broad, that unrolls like a panorama above the shoreline of the White Loch. Scholarly references to Scotland's traditional castles and tower houses abound: bartizans—a native speciality—sprout from every corner, crowstepping defines each gable end, battlements top the formidable tower. And then there are the French flourishes—the high-pitched pavilion roofs and the dormer pediments, not unlike their chic forebears at the House of the Binns (see pages 13–29). Inside and out, Lochinch is steeped in French and Scottish taste. Louisa Stair's father, the last duc de Coigny, died while the house was being built and her inheritance of monumental paintings and tapestries dictated the scale of various rooms. The aptness of the union is summed up by the close hanging of the martial portraits of the second Earl of Stair and the first duc de Coigny, who fought against each other in the 1743 campaign of the War of the Austrian Succession. Love, finally, conquers all.

The military gene remains a powerful dynamic in the family, as the weaponry and colours (regimental flags) displayed in the house demonstrate. All four successors of the tenth earl have served in the army and participated in most major conflicts of the twentieth century. The present earl, Jamie Stair, fought as a newly commissioned officer in the Scots Guards at the Battle of Mount Tumbledown in the Falklands War.

He left the army to help his father run Lochinch and inherited the title in 1996. " Managing an estate is a series of challenges and opportunities which are all consuming and very rewarding," he says. "There's no manual. It's a combination of business, heritage, history, and obligation." Emily Stair, whose parents rescued their family house, Stonor Park, is clear eyed about the challenges. "It did make it more daunting," she says. One of their greatest responsibilities is the continual restoration and maintenance of the garden, which John and Louisa Stair had not only rescued but transformed, thanks to the Victorian plant-hunting boom—and the mild climate—into one of the finest gardens for rhododendrons, pines, and other exotic species in the land. The family's guardianship of the garden, spanning more than three hundred years, is testament to their shared commitment in nurturing this patch of paradise in distant Wigtownshire.

PRECEDING PAGES: *The White Loch of Inch (far right), the Black Loch (far left).*

OPPOSITE: *The round pond.*

ABOVE: *Ruins of Castle Kennedy, focal point of the eighteenth-century formal garden.*

OVERLEAF: *Rhododendron walk.*

Monzie Castle

PERTHSHIRE

Lorimer's solution to the rebuilding of Monzie is archetypically Scottish. He was an artist, like so many of his race, with a split personality: on the one hand the introvert, drawn to the enclosed world of the tower house; on the other, the extrovert, fluent in the language of the great European tradition, as expressed in the luxury and sophistication of Monzie's principal block, as though the contemporaneous Ritz Hotel had been set down in a beautiful Perthshire glen.

In April 1908 the tenants of Monzie Castle in Perthshire were having lunch when the butler informed them that the house was in flames. The chimney in the servants' hall was prone to catching fire, but until then it had always fizzled out. This time it was different, and the butler announced that they ought to withdraw, as the fire was taking hold. "It was pretty cataclysmic," says Mrs. Isla Crichton, chatelaine of Monzie. "The chimney ran up the centre of the house and the roof just plunged into the middle. Almost everything was destroyed apart from two suits of armour."

Meanwhile the absent laird of Monzie, Charles Maitland Makgill Crichton, had only just arrived back in Britain from his house in California and was meeting up with his wife, Sybil, in a hotel in Brighton. Walking into the hotel, he was handed a telegram bringing news of the conflagration. The laird rushed off, but Sybil stayed behind, and a fellow guest turned to her and said: "The man you need is Robert Lorimer." It was the best piece of advice anyone could have given an Edwardian lady laird with a gutted castle to rebuild. The Edinburgh architect Robert Lorimer, who had just turned forty, was poised to reinvigorate Scottish vernacular architecture through a series of major country house commissions, placing him on a par with Edwin Lutyens in England. "Fortunately," says Isla Crichton,

"Monzie was well insured and Lorimer was duly instructed to rebuild Monzie within its surviving walls, with all the conveniences of electricity, central heating, and up-to-date plumbing." As *Country Life* dryly commented on Monzie's reconstruction: "Fire can never be anything but an enemy, but full insurance and wisdom in reconstruction are, to say the least, cheerful compensations."

Monzie (pronounced Munee), which in Scottish Gaelic means "field of corn," sits

PRECEDING PAGES: *High drama: cantilevered staircase and pedimented doorway into the drawing room.*

OPPOSITE: *Doric splendor of the hall. The columns are made from granolith, a form of concrete, to deter fire.*

TOP: *Architect Robert Lorimer, plans to hand, putting his best foot forward.*

ABOVE: *The gutted castle, 1908.*

BELOW: *Side elevation of Paterson's 1797 fort, dwarfing the 1634 tower house.*

OPPOSITE: *French Revival drawing room with Whytock and Reid settees; the Georgian fireplace, although damaged, survived the fire.*

OVERLEAF: *The eighteenth-century-designed landscape.*

in a sprawling valley dotted with evidence of prehistoric habitation, including a stone circle and Iron Age forts. The first modern dwelling was a seventeenth-century tower house with a date stone of 1634, built by the Graham family, who suffered badly in the Civil War. The next owners were a branch of the Campbells from the neighboring glen. Their legacy was the massive oblong castle, commissioned in 1797 from architect John Paterson, who had served as Robert Adam's clerk of works. A fortune made in India paid for it. The modern structure was built slam against the east wall of the tower house, with the result that the latter appears to cower beneath the mighty fort. The Campbells sold the castle in 1858 to the Johnstons, another family rich with Indian money and estates in Fife. It was a lure to tempt their wayward son back from Paris, but he took one look from his carriage and headed straight back to

the Continent. The house eventually passed by descent to the Johnstons' kinsmen the Maitland Makgill Crichtons, whose bloodlines have coursed through Scottish history, entitling them to the chiefdom of the Clan Crichton.

The twentieth-century story of the castle opens in 1902 with the arrival of the young laird Charles Maitland MakGill Crichton, recently married to Sybil Earle, the daughter of a distinguished London legal family. But they scarcely lived there, as their son contracted tuberculosis, from which he eventually died. In search of clear air, they decamped to California, buying a house and large ranch in Santa Barbara. The rebuilding of Monzie, completed in 1911, did not keep them in Scotland. The house, which was empty of furniture and fittings, was let to a Canadian millionaire, H. J. Scott, who gave Lorimer carte blanche to decorate and furnish

RIGHT: *Day nursery in the old tower house; the fireplace is hung with Dutch tiles.*

BELOW: *The fireplace's keystone is carved in the seventeenth-century manner.*

OPPOSITE: *Lorimer's oval drawing room incorporates Paterson's original hemicycle.*

OVERLEAF: *The "Wrenaissance" dining room, an homage to England's foremost seventeenth-century architect, Christopher Wren.*

it. However, he spent only two shooting seasons at Monzie before falling victim to the 1913 slump in America and never returned, nor did he claim his furniture, which, along with the original carpets and curtains, remains in the house today.

Charles and Sybil returned to Scotland just before the outbreak of World War I. The laird joined up and was killed at the Battle of Loos; his wife moved into Monzie nonetheless, part of which became a recuperation home for wounded officers. After the war the house was let again while the laird's widow and her children commuted between Brighton and California. "Grandma didn't like California, so in about 1920 she offloaded it," Isla Crichton recalls. "The person who bought the house also decided to buy the ranch. He was Mr. Paul Getty. The ranch became the site of his first oil well, which was still gushing in the 1960s. My husband and I visited some years ago: half of it was downtown Santa Barbara." The stoical Isla Crichton concludes this sorry tale by advising, "Looking back at lost opportunities is pointless."

Monzie was largely let between the wars, but in 1938 Isla Crichton's parents-in-law took possession, and despite the disruption of the war, the house became the permanent home of the family. Isla Crichton and her husband, Charles, moved in in 1979. "I'm just plain Mrs. Crichton now," she says, "as we drop a barrel every generation."

On being met at the front door by Isla Crichton, one is led quickly across the dark hall and through a door into the original tower house. This is where her tour begins—and the genius of Robert Lorimer is first revealed. Brought up at Kellie Castle in Fife, which he helped his father restore, Lorimer was steeped in the aesthetic of traditional Scottish architecture. A devotee of William Morris's belief in the "union of the arts," he built up a team of stonemasons, metalworkers, woodcarvers, and plasterers to realize his vision of a modern vernacular style. His internal reconstruction of the tower house plays on the age-old functions of shelter and comfort. A winding stair leads to the family quarters, principally the day

nursery, which features a wide fireplace, seventeenth century in scale, hung with old Dutch tiles. Every detail of this homely room was crafted with simplicity and common sense: iron spirals as the catches to shutters, simple elm paneling, and built-in cupboards, all painted in Lorimer's favored palette of moss greens and pale blues, reflecting the tones of Scotland.

Lorimer's affectionate evocation of Scottish domesticity is no preparation for his next trick. Stepping through an unassuming tongue-and-groove door, one emerges mid-flight on a soaring, cantilevered staircase with a delicate eighteenth-century French balustrade; below is the Roman-columned hall, above is a giant door case jutting out into the landing from angled walls, its broken pediment touching the ceiling with a note of baroque defiance. A master of the Belle Époque is at work, one who can fill the void of Paterson's geometric fort with a series of elegant spaces in different styles and moods: an oval Louis XV drawing room, a Christopher Wren dining room, a circular Art Nouveau card room (in a turret). All are furnished with pieces—many designed by Lorimer himself—supplied by the leading Edinburgh decorator, Whytock and Reid. Lorimer's taste is present in every detail. "Just as a ship must have a Captain," he wrote, ". . . it is essential that the architect should have a definitive say regarding all the decorative work that is put into his building." Monzie was the first commission on which he controlled every aspect of the interior decoration, down to the last fringe and tassel. When the interiors of so many other Lorimer houses have been degraded and their contents dispersed, its survival offers unique documentation of his art and craft.

Lorimer's solution to the rebuilding of Monzie is archetypically Scottish. He was an artist, like so many of his race, with a split

personality: on the one hand the introvert, drawn to the enclosed world of the tower house; on the other, the extrovert, fluent in the language of the great European tradition, as expressed in the luxury and sophistication of Monzie's principal block, as though the contemporaneous Ritz Hotel had been set down in a beautiful Perthshire glen.

"Charles and I always realised we had something a bit different from anyone else," Isla Crichton says. "We always thought that it would never come into fashion until Lorimer had been dead for a hundred years—and there's still some time to go, as he died in 1929." Monzie in its untouched state is all the evidence one needs to elevate Lorimer to the Scottish pantheon.

OPPOSITE: CLOCKWISE FROM TOP LEFT, *Lorimer plasterwork, Georgian caryatid, and a swag from a chimneypiece that survived the fire.*

TOP: *Staircase oculus.*

ABOVE: *Neo-baroque entrance to the drawing room.*

OVERLEAF: *The valley of Monzie, meaning "field of corn" in Scottish Gaelic.*

SELECTED BIBLIOGRAPHY

GENERAL

The Buildings of Scotland. Pevsner Architectural Guides. 12 vols. New Haven and London: Yale University Press, 1979–present.

Dunbar, John G. *The Architecture of Scotland*. London: B. T. Batsford, 1978.

Glendinning, Miles, and Aonghus MacKechnie. *Scottish Architecture*. World of Art Series. London: Thames & Hudson, 2004.

Gow, Ian, and Alistair, Rowan, eds. *Scottish Country Houses 1600–1914*. Edinburgh: Edinburgh University Press, 1995.

Macaulay, James. *The Classical Country House in Scotland 1660–1800*. London: Faber and Faber, 1987.

Walker, David M. "Dictionary of Scottish Architects" (database maintained by Historic Scotland), www.scottisharchitects.org.uk

HOUSE OF THE BINNS

Dalyell, Sir James, and James Beveridge. "Inventory of the Plenishing of the House of the Binns at the Date of the Death of General Thomas Dalyell." *Proceedings of the Society of Antiquaries of Scotland*, vol. 58, Fifth series–vol 10, 1924.

Dalyell, Kathleen. "Living in the Past." *Prospect*, no. 59 (Spring 1996).

Dalyell, Kathleen, and Tam Dalyell. *House of the Binns*. National Trust for Scotland Guidebook. Edinburgh: National Trust for Scotland, 2011.

Howard, Deborah. *Scottish Architecture: Reformation to Restoration 1560–1660*. Edinburgh: Edinburgh University Press, 1995.

Waterson, Merlin. *A Noble Thing: The National Trust and Its Benefactors*. London: Scala, 2011.

BALCASKIE

Anstruther, A. W. *The History of the Family of Anstruther*. Edinburgh and London: William Blackwood & Sons, 1923.

"Balcaskie." *Country Life*, March 2, 1912.

Fitzalan-Howard, Philip. "Balcaskie House, Fife, and the Early Architecture of Sir William Bruce." Master's thesis, University of St Andrews, ref: ThNA998.B8F5H7.

MacKechnie, Aonghus. "Sir William Bruce: 'The Chief Introducer of Architecture in This Country.'" *Proceedings of the Society of Antiquaries of Scotland*, vol. 132, 2002, pp. 499–519.

Wemyss, Charles. "A Study of Aspiration and Ambition: The Scottish Treasury Commission and Its Impact upon the Development of Scottish Country House Architecture 1667–1682." Ph.D. diss., University of Dundee, December 2008. Accessed at discoverydundee.ac.uk.

DRUMLANRIG

Colvin, H. M. "A Scottish Origin for English Palladianism." *Architectural History*, vol. 17, 1974.

Girouard, Mark. "Drumlanrig Castle, Dumfriesshire" I, II, and III. *Country Life*, August 23, 1960; September 1, 1960; September 8, 1960.

Scott, John Montagu Douglas. *Drumlanrig: The Castle, Its People and Its Paintings*. The Buccleuch Estates, 2010.

ARNISTON

"Arniston, Midlothian: The Seat of Lady Dundas." *Country Life*, August 15 and 22, 1925.

Dundas-Bekker, Althea. *Arniston Remembered*. Arniston, n.d.

Fleming, John. *Robert Adam and His Circle in Edinburgh and Rome*. London: John Murray, 1962.

Fry, Michael. *The Dundas Despotism*. Edinburgh: John Donald, 2004.

Omond, George W. T. *The Arniston Memoirs: Three Centuries of a Scottish House 1571–1838, Edited from the Family Papers*. Edinburgh: David Douglas, 1887.

Tait, A. A. "William Adam and Sir John Clerk: Arniston and 'The Country Seat.'" *Burlington Magazine*, vol. III, no. 792, 1969.

FOULIS CASTLE

Munro, Mr. and Mrs. Patrick. "The Munros of Foulis and Foulis Castle." Foulis, n.d.

DUMFRIES HOUSE

Binney, Marcus, Sir Hugh Roberts, and Charlotte Rostek. *Dumfries House: The Great Steward of Scotland's Dumfries House Trust*. London: Leighton Printing, 2011.

Dumfries House: A Chippendale Commission. 2 vols. Auction catalogues, Christie's London, July 12–13, 2007. London: Christie's, 2007.

Fleming, John. *Robert Adam and His Circle in Edinburgh and Rome*. London: John Murray, 1962.

BOWHILL

Bowhill. Selkirk: The Buccleuch Heritage Trust, 1999.

Cornforth, John. "Bowhill, Selkirk." *Country Life*, June 5, 12, 19, and 26, 1975.

Girouard, Mark. *The Victorian Country House*. New Haven and London: Yale University Press, 1979.

BALLINDALLOCH

Macpherson-Grant Russell, Clare. *I Love Food*. Peterborough: Heritage House Group, 2004.

——. *Ballindalloch Castle: Romantic Pearl of the North & Highland Home of the Lairds of Ballindalloch*. Peterborough: Heritage House Group, 2011.

Holloway, James. *The Great Houses of Scotland*. Edinburgh: National Galleries of Scotland, 2002.

LOCHINCH

"Lochinch." *Country Life*, December 29, 1900.

"Lochinch." *Country Life*, September 22, 1934.

Wainwright, Clive. *The Romantic Interior: The British Collector at Home, 1750–1850*. New Haven and London: Yale University Press, 1989.

MONZIE

Hussey, Christopher. *The Work of Sir Robert Lorimer, K.B.E., A.R.A., R.S.A.* London: Country Life Limited, 1931.

"Modern Scottish Architecture: The Work of Sir Robert Lorimer." Architectural Supplement to *Country Life*, September 27, 1913.

Montgomery-Massingberd, Hugh. "Monzie and the Crichtons." *The Field*, November 30, 1985.

Savage, Peter. *Lorimer and the Edinburgh Craft Designers*. Edinburgh: Paul Harris Publishing, 1980.

Dedicated to members of the next generation

William Fennell and

Bryce Knox and Constance Knox

ACKNOWLEDGMENTS

First my gratitude goes to photographer James Fennell, whose response to the houses and landscape, and insistence on working only in natural light—no easy feat when days shorten in Scotland—has resulted in such beautiful and atmospheric images.

I would like to thank His Royal Highness the Prince of Wales, titled in Scotland the Duke of Rothesay, and the trustees of the Great Steward of Scotland's Dumfries House Trust for permission to photograph Dumfries House.

I would also like to thank (ranked according to the period of their houses) Tam and Kathleen Dalyell; Toby Anstruther of that Ilk and Kate Anstruther; the Duke and Duchess of Buccleuch and Queensberry (for Drumlanrig and Bowhill); Mrs Althea Dundas-Bekker and Henrietta Dundas-Bekker; Hector Munro of Foulis, Chief of the Clan Munro, and Mrs Patrick Munro of Foulis; Clare Macpherson-Grant Russell and Oliver Russell; the Earl and Countess of Stair; and Mrs Isla Crichton—all of whom have extended hospitality to myself and James Fennell and shown unstinting generosity in answering innumerable questions about their houses and their family histories.

My thanks also go to Mark Atkinson, June Baxter, Ann Buchanan, the Marquess of Bute, Emily Cherrington, Professor Peter Davidson, Michael Davis, Michael Fawcett, Philip Fitzalan-Howard, Richard and Virginia Fyffe, Mark Gibson, John Goffin, Khalil Hafiz Khairallah, Laura Lindsay, Todd Longstaffe-Gowan, William Lorimer, Moira Mackenzie and Maia Sheridan of Special Collections, St Andrews University, Rebecca Parker, Sir Hugh Roberts, Charlotte Rostek, James Ruggles-Brise, Julio Soriano-Ruiz, the Hon James Stourton, Benjamin Tindall, Jamie and Sarah Troughton, Timothy Wilcox, and William Zachs.

Additional thanks to the National Trust for Scotland, Harriet Anstruther of Harriet Anstruther Studio for her assistance in styling the photographs of Balcaskie, and the staffs of the London Library and the library of the Royal Commission on the Ancient and Historical Monuments of Scotland.

Collette Hutchinson, Andrew Stanley, Karim White, and Laura Willis at Thames & Hudson have been an enormous support in publishing the book in the United Kingdom.

The greatest debt is to my friend and publisher in New York, Mark Magowan of Vendome Press, who first proposed the idea, and to my editor, Jackie Decter, and designer, Patricia Fabricant; all deserve huge thanks for their vision and enthusiasm at every stage of the book's production.

Finally, four cognoscenti set me on the right path with lists of their favourite houses. They are: Hugh Buchanan, Ian Gow, James Holloway, and Cindy, Lady Shaw Stewart. Their suggestions were an inspiration. Charles Wemyss provided me with invaluable information on Sir William Bruce and his patrons. And as always, my wife, Caroline, deserves a medal for her patience and encouragement, as well as for joining me on our adventures across Scotland on the trail of Scottish country houses.

—JAMES KNOX

First published in the United States of America in 2012 by
The Vendome Press
1334 York Avenue
New York, NY 10021
www.vendomepress.com

ISBN 978-0-86565-288-0

Editor: Jacqueline Decter
Production Editor: Alecia Reddick
Designer: Patricia Fabricant

Library of Congress Cataloging-in-Publication Data

Knox, James, author.
The Scottish country house / James Knox ; photographs by James Fennell.
pages cm
Includes bibliographical references.
ISBN 978-0-86565-288-0
1. Country homes--Scotland. I. Fennell, James, illustrator. II. Title.
NA7334.K58 2012
728'.3709411--dc23
2012011407

Printed by Toppan Printing Co., Ltd. in China
First printing